THE COLLECTED POEMS
OF PADRAIC FALLON

'Head of My Father': Bust in stainless steel by Conor Fallon.
Photograph: Conor Fallon, courtesy of The Arts Council, Ireland /
An Chomhairle Ealaíon.

PADRAIC FALLON

Collected Poems

introduction by Seamus Heaney
edited, with an afterword and notes
by Brian Fallon

CARCANET
GALLERY

Padraic Fallon's *Collected Poems*
are first published
simultaneously in paperback
and in a clothbound edition
on 28 June 1990

Carcanet Press Limited
208-212 Corn Exchange Buildings
Manchester M4 3BQ

The Gallery Press
Loughcrew, Oldcastle
County Meath, Ireland

British Library Cataloguing in Publication Data
Fallon, Padraic
  Collected Poems.
  1. Poetry in English, 1900-1974 – Texts
  1. Title
  821'.912

  ISBN 0-85635-817-7 *(Carcanet)*
  ISBN 1-85235-052-0 *(Gallery paperback)*
  ISBN 1-85235-053-9 *(Gallery clothbound)*

Carcanet Press acknowledges financial assistance from
the Arts Council of Great Britain
The Gallery Press receives financial assistance from
An Chomhairle Ealaíon / The Arts Council, Ireland

Typeset in 10pt Palatino by Bryan Williamson, Darwen, Lancashire
Printed and bound in England by SRP Ltd., Exeter

Contents

LATE POEMS (1960-1974)

TRANSLATIONS AND VERSIONS OF HOMERIC HYMNS

9

Introduction

To drive across Ireland, east to west, towards Padraic Fallon's native County Galway, is to experience a double sensation of refreshment and *déjà-vu*. The refreshment comes from the big lift of the sky beyond the River Shannon, the *déjà-vu* from entering a landscape which has been familiar for a century as an image of the dream-Ireland invented by the Irish Literary Revival. Yet even a disenchanted critic, tired of exposing the mystifications of social and economic reality in that old Celtic Twilight of cottage and curragh, cannot fail to respond to vistas of stone-walled plains running to the horizon and shifting cloudscapes underlit from the Atlantic. For in spite of the west of Ireland's status as a country of myth, the actual place can still waken an appetite for experience that is pristine and unconstrained.

All this affected the climate of Padraic Fallon's mind and art. The market town of Athenry where he grew up was admittedly more down-to-earth than Yeats's Ballylee or Lady Gregory's Coole Park, yet Fallon began as a poet by taking on the protective colouring of the Ireland which those "last Romantics" had imagined. Its accents and its typical inhabitants appear, for example, in an early poem like "The Waistcoat". Nevertheless, the instructive thing about the Collected Poems is the spectacle it affords of a writer gradually and consciously negotiating his way through his influences and managing, with a mild but ineradicable self-confidence, to cultivate his own voice and his own subjects. Fallon's *oeuvre* can now be seen to stand in secure and complementary relation to the achievements of Austin Clarke and Patrick Kavanagh; but its "learned" tendency and later fitful Poundian impulses suggest that it was also susceptible to a modernist strain that entered Irish writing in the 1930s.

"Gurteen" was the first poem of Padraic Fallon's to make me take cognizance of the strength and importance of his work. It arrived when I was editing an issue of *Soundings*, the annual round-up of new Irish poetry which Blackstaff Press published for a while in the early 1970s, and it was the first part of the triptych, "Three Houses" (p.144). Before that, I had known Fallon's poems only slightly, from seeing them in the standard anthologies; but nothing which I had read ever brought me to my senses in quite the same way as these low-key, sure-footed stanzas:

11

I had no gift for it.
It hung out in the welter of the moor;
A black-faced country staring in

All day. Never did the sun
Explode with flowers in the dark vases
Of the windows. The fall was wrong

And there was uplifted the striking north
Before the door.
We lived in the flintlights of a cavern floor.

This was neither the "slack string" approach to writing advocated by Kavanagh in his later comic phase, nor did it belong with the more sardonic and resistant tones of the mature Austin Clarke. It issued from a sensibility more temperate than Kavanagh's and better tempered than Clarke's, and if it was less forcefully personal than their particular notes, it was all the more interesting for being the achieved freedom of a deliberate stylist.

"Gurteen" was a discovery and a resource, a manifestation of kindred spirit. It was not just that Fallon's "black-faced country" was instantly recognizable – the phrase is wide open but I saw the high-gloss, spade-marked faces of bog-banks. It was more that the natural pitch of voice in his lines managed to embody a recognizably indigenous note and yet remained at ease within the decorum of the English tradition. Here was a voice that had somehow freed itself of the slightly too colourful diction and too animated address which were the legacy of the Revival to the poets of Fallon's generation; and yet it had retained its original Irish accent.

There was an overall security of tone, an assumption of common ground and easy access between voice and audience. For example, the phrase, "The fall was wrong", was neither paraded as an Irishism – which it is not – nor clarified for the benefit of the outsider as a technical term – unnecessary anyhow, since one grasps that it has to do with the way the dark country at the window affected the angle at which light was permitted to enter the house. Moreover, tone was only one symptom of a self-possession that was grounded upon intimacy with a landscape and expressed itself in other purely linguistic ways, from that nice balance of casualness and declarativeness in the opening line, "I had no gift for it", to the half-conscious echo of Wordsworth's Westminster Bridge sonnet in the phrase, "Never did the sun...".

All of this came most carefully upon its hour in 1972 when political upheavals in Northern Ireland were pressing to the fore all over again old, unfashionable questions about the relationship between poetry, cultural heritage and national allegiance. A few months earlier, I had proposed a somewhat oversimplified programme for the poetry I thought I wanted to write. In an attempt to sail between the Scylla of "the Irish mode" originally sponsored by Thomas MacDonagh and maintained as a literary category by later writers such as Robert Farren in his book *The Course of Irish Verse* (1949), and the Charybdis of a more standardized, New Lines-ish, iambic English, I devised a conceit in which Irish experience was to equal vowels and the English literary tradition was to equal consonants, and my poems were to be "vocables adequate to my whole experience". It was, admittedly, a fairly Euphuistic conception, but even so, it did signal a genuine stylistic problem, one which has been endemic to Irish writing and whose solution always represents a definite moment in a poet's development. Fallon, obviously, had solved it and was enjoying an open channel to the workings of his own spirit – which workings Wordsworth rightly defined as the poet's true subject.

Yet this is to project too simply and too confidently upon the basis of a single poem. One has only to read "Shanballard", the second section of "Three Houses", to find the pure personal note – "the sun upon a breakfast knife" – being overcome by the rhapsodic strains of Dylan Thomas – "I / Was the crown prince of birds early / With the first cock crowing." In fact, even in Fallon's later poems, there is often a stylistic faltering. Sometimes it manifests itself as an over-absorbed ratiocination, so that the elaboration of the poem's argument grows too intent and the suppleness of natural speech rhythm gets hampered. All one has to do to feel the contrast between the natural weather of a sensibility and the uphill labour of a will is to read the first "Lost Man" (p.136), where the furniture of the poem is both part of the setting and an expression of the subject, and then read "Lost Man in Me" (p.141), where arguments and allusions are being reached for beyond the emotional circumference of the poem itself.

Obviously this is not to claim that argument cannot work as a poetic procedure, or that extravagant allusion necessarily constitutes a threat to a poem's integrity. Not at all. Indeed, one of Fallon's notable contributions to Irish poetry is the way he establishes wonderful, far-flung relations between the bog-bank and the Buddha, between the byre and *The Golden Bough*. A poem like "Totem" has an eerie, risky originality about it, exercising mythological consciousness in a completely un-Yeatsian way, and treating an experience common in the life of the small farm world depicted by Patrick Kavanagh in an idiom very different from Kavanagh's:

> They knew it, the Totem people, the world
> Inside the world where man
> Makes metaphors
> For the animal.

Such classical and legendary paralleling is most successful when Fallon keeps his grip on the actuality of his experience. It is because the reeks and textures of known places have been rendered in "A Visit West", "The Head" and "The Small Town of John Coan" that I find them more persuasive than poems like "Boyne Valley" and "Magna Mater". These latter seem to push their luck much too far into the field of abstraction.

This mythic side of Fallon's work is all of a piece with his translations. In the Greek material in particular, such as his versions of "Hylas" by Theocritus, Pindar's "The Stealing of Apollo's Cattle", Hesiod's "The Muses' Gift" and the Homeric hymn "To Pan", he manages another way of rhyming the remembered facts of Irish rural life with the venerable texts, and produces translations that not only conjure a sense of their originals but also spring-clean our vision of the natural world and clarify the ear. Ezra Pound obviously helped him to find his note, but there is a native tin whistle plainly audible behind the classical Pan-pipes.

There would also appear to be a vital connection between the open, sudden mode of those translations and the quickly articulated, dramatically timed utterance of some of the best late poems. "Dardanelles 1916" and "A Bit of Brass" look simple, which is part of their strength. But it is a condition of simplicity which has cost the poet a lifetime of imaginative effort, and it reminds one again that when it comes to the expression of new subject matter in poetry, formal and stylistic considerations are automatically involved. The Irish soldier in British Army uniform, en route for the Great War, was once a common sight but he has nevertheless rarely occurred in books of verse; and before Fallon could "get it in", he had spent the best part of a career working through and working out subjects that were traditionally sanctioned and more immediately current in the literary ambience of Ireland during the 1930s and 1940s.

In his "Afterword" to the *Collected Poems*, Brian Fallon writes that many of his father's generation were very conscious that they "were 'Irish Irish' in contrast to the predominant Anglo-Irishness of their predecessors." His account of the imaginative consequences of this awareness, and of the general cultural and intellectual conditions which then prevailed, constitutes the background to the poems of Padraic Fallon's early and middle period. In them, as a prelude to his own gradually fulfilled vocation, Fallon rehearses many of the themes which had preoccupied Irish writers during the previous fifty years. His translations from the Irish of the rambling folk poet, Anthony Raftery, and his generally sympathetic response to the Gaelic heritage of Connacht would have found corroboration from his friend Austin Clarke; and the survivals of what the song called "spalpeen and jack" in the life of the countryside would have been urged on him as subject-matter by F.R. Higgins. Yet it is also worth emphasizing Brian Fallon's reminder that the poet was highly aware of the gap between literary conventions and the life of the country, and drawing attention once again to the wry coda he delivers on all these matters in "For Paddy Mac":

> No poets I knew of; or they mouthed each other's words;
> Such low powered gods
> They died, as they were born, in byres.

And then, of course, came Yeats; and at first sight it might seem that Fallon's attitude to him was the same as Nodier's to Malherbe, "qui aurait pu, sans grand inconvénient, se dispenser de venir." In Padraic Fallon's big addresses to the bard, there is a wonderful mixture of awe and shyness as he attempts to establish his own poetic and political freehold in a territory where Yeats is still demanding the ground rents. Robert Garrett has noted the "ventriloquism" of these performances, in particular the poem "Yeats's Tower at Ballylee", and diagnosed the condition of imaginative stalemate of which they are symptoms; yet the canon is nicely completed by the posthumous addition to it of these poems which reveal one of the big dynamics of Irish literary history in the post-Yeatsian era. If, as John Montague famously remarked, "Kavanagh liberated us but he liberated us into ignorance", we are now in a position to add the corollary that "Fallon re-educated us towards what we knew".

These poems have the full dress and the high step of set pieces. They are indeed analogous to certain time-honoured parades that occur every year in some towns in Northern Ireland, where the

Orange bands march provocatively close to the Nationalist areas. They carry the banner of difference, the note of resistance and the boast of triumph into range of the enemy. Yet for all their panoply and glamour, they are based on anxiety, and reveal rather than resolve a tension.

The Yeats series constitutes such a pageant. The poems have a fine solemnity about them and a real sense of historical occasion, and they are a gift to any critic reading Irish poetry within an Oedipal, Bloomean framework. Fallon indeed cannot get an equal footing upon the historic Galway ground until he breaks up his Yeatsian lines and stanzas, not in order to weep but to admit the broken lives of the inmates of Ballinasloe Lunatic Asylum; and to admit also the vertiginous disjunctions between himself as aspiring schoolboy, nose pressed to the big sweetshop window of classical learning, and the remote, apotheosized sage of Bally-lee. Which is why "Stop on the Road to Ballylee", for all its obscurities and private associations (and in spite of an ill-judged last line), seems to me the triumph of the series:

> Three measures
> Of clay and we're at liberty to leave
> To lay our tin wreaths on more iambic matter
> At the Big Tower (those centenaries)
> In Ballylee, Ballylee.

Once again, Ezra Pound would appear to have been the influence that opened the path and allowed Fallon to draw new breath, although it would be a mistake to enlist Fallon's work in general into the Poundian line. His sense of form remained too intimate with traditional conceptions of harmony and logical structure, and his ear too responsive to the old tunes of verse-writing for Pound's kind of modernism to take him over.

Yet it is in the many breaks with what was habitual to him that Fallon established his most memorable claim upon the disinterested reader. In addition to the work I have mentioned, consider the surprise riches of "A Flask of Brandy", the exhilaration of renewal in "An Island", and these lucent, opulent stanzas which conclude the late "Painting of My Father":

> Land's End some few miles away; the tide
> Is white round the Mount; a bird
> Stands on the sundial on the lawn; Spring
> Is hovering;

And in the tulip tree – hallucination – some
Medieval person reads a tome

(To disappear battered
By a rainshower with his
Monkshood, creature of air;
The bird stays on, real enough;
A woodpecker)

A country ironed out
Into saints and menhirs where
You never put a foot,

Where the weather camps an hour before
It stamps the soft shires, taking over
The whole south of England at a blow.

These lines offer a passage towards new poetic conditions; they
are at ease and posthumous to the old cultural, linguistic and
historical anxieties. Enlivening, accessible, proof of the examined
life and the generous instinct, empowered by impulse and un-
regulated by programmes, they are conducive to the next move
of the spirit and the art. They remind us, in fact, of what the best
work in this book demonstrates: that Padraic Fallon comes to us
now as much a contemporary as he was when he began.

SEAMUS HEANEY

Early Poems
(1930-1945)

To a Woodpigeon

(for J.M.C.)

Though I was told that in a speckled wood,
Most matronly, your flickering legs
Cradled in their soft twilights a gentle brood
Or the clutched lights of eggs,
You were no bird at all to me when I
Was young, and had the skies to breathe
But Beauty, passing, lost in their own blue cry
In the rich distances of Meath.

Then on a day of wind when I exultantly
Clamoured with the elements as though I were
Storm with lightnings forking from my fingers,
I saw you topple from the air
In the hawk's foot and had not a single thought
Of pity for you then, so utterly did my being
Lean to the strong, the proud athletic ones
Who take like kings their prey upon the wing.

Praise the strong, the violent whose will is energy!
Yet, when in a mist of the growing wheat
My coming scared the brazen bird,
Your torn body, vaguely threshing feet,
Upturned in a silver scattering of wild plumes
Suddenly seemed so piteous that I
Was bitter for a moment as though all beauty hung
In the bale of a yellow eye.

Bitter while your last life told the cold beads
Of your eyes; and after that
Pitiful for all under a ramping foot.
Oh! sound your soft horn now for there I met
As ghosts on the heart's far borders those worth my praise,
Christ, Prometheus,
And the bright kin who, bringing sweet destinies to the small,
Were nailed on a cross.

Long John

'On yellow crowns and purples, I
Might stake the good purse of my soul,
But if the bad luck turned the wheel,'
   Said the tramper John Mulroy,
'The devil might get me in the heel:
So on this sunny hill I'll roll,
My long knees wandering up the sky,
And think while clouds drift through my knees
That no crown weighs a moment's ease.

'O! if I had that ruddy One
Who queened in Cruachan long ago
And loved all gambling gallant men,'
   Cried the rambler John,
'I'd have the great times in Mayo.
But stay! would I be happier then?
For would my work be ever done
In keeping off the other men;
And think! O white cloud on my knee!
Of that responsibility.'

'Now that the young year's spun her coin
Into the sun and speckled bees
Hive the dripping summer here,'
   Yawned that rascal John,
'The noise of farming in the leas
Is pleasing to a drowsy ear,
And as I stretch out I must own
That hives and farmers shut my eyes
As well as mother's lullabies.'

Gillies of Song

(to F.R. Higgins)

Now the last herds are tallied for the seas,
Taking the thunder from the grasses here,
And each cold bush has cast its blackbird, we
Find old Meath hushed in many silences:
But climbing up into the last green air
Of Tara, suddenly
We find an errant day of Summer's days
Lost here above five provinces of haze.

Here with the skies about us, memories
Rebuild in grass the flowering oak and bronze
That tucked blue counties under a kingly arm,
Wild clans and wandering harps about its knees,
And queens whose profiles lingering on coins
Of dream still delicately charm
Hard seasons as the robin's autumn ghost
Pulls thin sweet reels of music from the frost.

We are lost out of time while this gold cock of a sun
Struts to the noon as though about to crow
To some young moon that he remembers here;
And softly, softly over roads grassgrown
The old hours stir again; big horsemen go
To guesting-house and beer;
Honey is hiving in Summer, salmon from the weirs
Come, creeling the silver Boyne in sally osiers.

The heart would take like grass lost music from that air
Of ancient summer, gathering old slow tune
Quiet as the dewy drifting of the grass,
But day scarce turns on a wild bright side before
Her cloudy elbow knocks the sun from noon
And in tossed haze we pass
To thinking how wild blossom, bole and root
Was broken under a cleric's heavy foot.

O let us sing, my friend, while low trees cassock light
In saintlike tonsures; though the glitter's gone
From the bone and our leaves take to withered heels
We still have song enough to put a blight

Of song on those black saints who took the moon
Of Ireland from the hills
Of Faery with bells and had her whipped,
Candled and cursed until she turned harelipped.

Though Ruadhan won, we'll toss the coin again
And call the tune in Inns where drovers sit
Above the smoke. When dreams are fiery
Among the cups, we'll loosen that old reign
Of Gold into our age and praising it
The slender Moon of Faery
Will glitter up the reaches, wild, alone
With the sweet secret music of her bone.

Wisdom

Who'd love again on this old rambling star
Where love, cast out of God's harem,
Grows coarse in the weather over a gypsy fire
Of stick and cowdung? Who, having coming to sense,
Tenting with her but comes to know
As mere illusions
Those dark eyes heavy with dream
Of lost kingdoms,
The sound of strings and drums
She carries about her soft in the air as echo?
Having won at length to wisdom, who'd wish to know
Once more an empty fallen queen of Pharaoh?

Bear with me then. I, that was hunter once,
Guess rightly that you have as many dewy
Turnings as a hare; but having come to sense
I know the glittering ancient self in you
Is not for dog and horn. So you may stay
As a sitting hare in the dew
Quietly assembling the moon in each cold eye,
Unless in folly I find
Like Solomon a second wind
And on this falling star seek more than a dog's day,
Running with that old stager who lived and died in the faith
That the crown of love is . . . to be in at the death.

From "Lady Day"

In the low house whose thick lights
Laboured each day to take true casts of her
Brown face with its thin high bones, she washed before the fire
Like a queen in a penny:
And there as she did her hair in an old green glass
Her face bloomed delicately as a reed
Dropping cold seeds of lakewater while over her the dead
Framed in their Sunday finery
Were drawn from the shadows and gilded till they burned on
    the walls
Like calendars for some sad purgatory.

And there as she stepped from one dress into another
In the tremors and rays of
A reverie as quietly electric as the Great Emperor Moth's
One feared that the men for miles
Would arrive with beating hands at the little window
Out of the stirring countryside;
But nothing happened; demurely she steps out with
A maid's mouth and a maid's eyes
Past hens asleep in their feathers and a sow in a fat grunt
And cycles off into the skies.

And the slow afternoon big and blue
Lifted in hazy heckles from her shoulders;
Moving, she trailed the sky too
Over crops and cattle;
And out of the ripening fields which she spread
Like a peacock's tail, so very small in
That huge plumage of smoky country, she
Advances to the Pattern;
Her black hair combed to the scalp
Brilliant as oil on water.

She picked a calm way through
Mourners and merrymakers where I waited
With the airs haymaking softly on the new
Mown graves of the parish dead,
And there as promised I sought her among the neighbours –
To find in group after group her twin instead,

O sequence of sisters! O cool stone shedding comets!
Wherever my dazzled eye stayed
Some girl in her very image stared at me and smiled
With the same red mouth, brown eyes, and small black head.

Writing on the Wall

Throw something to the gulls, any old scrap
As you go down the quays when day awakes!
Throw something to the gulls, they are so quiet, so keen,
In those soft moments when the dawn breaks
With a soft feathery explosion.

Anything, a bit of unblessed bread, throw it
To the gulls, throw something to the gulls.
Though they seem dropped bright feathers of dawn, a poet
Knows better. They are no eddying snowflakes
But bellies, appetites.

Throw something then, a pennyweight of bread!
Before one preying beak can gather it between
Wind and water, thousands are round your head,
A tumult, a squawking crown, wind-blown;
You are caught in a storm.

Cast your bread upon those waters, it will return
In a foam of birds that scrawls upon the air
A luminous word that will leave you insecure
Wondering how belly-hunger with this quill of rain and storm
Could forge such a dazzling signature.

Consubstantiality

If heredity
Indeed determine history,
Helen, through her known bird's blood and Troy sticks
Burning, could well account herself the Phoenix.

But how shall I guess
At my father at all and his business
If I know only my mother and the long griefs
Of her four beautiful green leaves?

What shall I know of him, my milk-teeth won
At your quiet paps, unless I follow on
As the caterpillar clambers through his own rings
Suddenly to come on wings?

If father's thumb need
Luck or not, his image, a large dream, haunts his seed;
This kinship then is the blood's philosophy
And, followed, home, enlarges me.

I admit your motherhood –
My mouth is sweet with it – but is the male blood
And mind to be denied which also I inherited,
And your great lover discredited?

Then bid me lady,
Stretch my boy's to a man's body,
And finding the new huge trick,
Engage you in a larger rhetoric.

For there's no glory in a house,
Where the master's absent, if his son's a mouse
Among the spinning wheels; think of my shame
If one day he came home

Out of the sea's tumult roping
The heaven's great song ashore, and I moping
Among the spitting suitors at the fire,
Field and cupboard nearly bare.

Could I offer in excuse
This love that makes me envious
Of time, the slow great stream, because it floats
Your murmuring wide leaves and drifts with your roots,

When this love so disperses me
Like vague air over your vegetable scenery
To tell like little steeples the sweet innumerable names
Of your small cities in my hazy palms?

No. Let the great bright bow
Stand upon the cloudy wall and bid me go
Seek him through blood and sweat, and fashion from the way
An heroic body for the Judgement Day.

Lest, when the bow is bent,
He not recognize me in that summary moment
And I go down, too, with the rest before the whistling string,
A nothing to drift in nothing.

I must be about his business
For he comes so near my earth our various substances
Seem one, as trembling from the dim cocoon
The butterfly is dazzled leaf and sun.

The Waistcoat

Oro, the islandmen
Load herring from the white shoals
Into the barrows of the shawled fishwives
On the grey wall of Galway:
And lightly where sunlight was warehoused by the water
From the tarred hulls they sway
In their blue homespuns and skin shoes
To the hazy wall and away.

O tell me what lazy Peeler
Thumbing his girth will dare them
Now money that ripens like rain on ropes
Runs down their hasty fingers?
And what fat terrified son of the devil
That tends a till won't pull back porter
All night for men whose eyes make knives
Of the lights that worm through his bottled windows?

But quietly at last as a sheep-fair
From the old square the day disperses,
One spark of the sun stands hitched
Like a lonely ram in a corner,

And Padraic the son of Patcheen Rua
Shakes the drink from the wild top of his skull
And stoops from the door in his whispering shoes
To dandle the sky on his shoulder.

O grey city
Of stone and mist and water,
Here's terror, a son of Clan Flaherty
Footloose in your sleepy air.
Have you no shocked sudden memory
Of rape and ringing steeple
As he grows in a lane, towering, till the sea
Seems no more size than a mackerel?

Fly for the bishop, quick.
Call all the lazy constables for, O,
By Padraic Patcheen Rua now
An innocent woman idles.
Bright in the midnight of her shawl
Her face rises, in her own light
Her piled hair slipping from the comb
Could hide a lover out of sight.

O, Padraic Patcheen Rua, such a woman
Never had a match
In any thatched house on the windy island;
And, O, Padraic, did she stretch
On the top of a headland with you of an evening
What riches your great hand would win
Burning on all her slow horizons down
From crown to shin.

Man, dear, do you dawdle
And the world before you?
A ship with two sails
And a gallow's crew,
And the wind right for Connemara
Where you will have your will
And potheen in a jug
By a three-legged stool?

Open your mouth, O dolt.
Strike the great silver string.
Give the gossips a story, we sicken
Of talking of tides and fish.
Lay hands on her, show her the rocks
And rainbows of water we twist
Out of ourselves for the women, taking
An ocean on the bowsprit.

Are you making a mock of us, Padraic?
Is an islandman backing
Round like a colt if a woman
But finger his elbow?
By God, do you turn and run
And she trying to hold you
So hard that you leave in her two hands
Three parts of your woollen waistcoat?

O, your wife will magnify you
To our wives at the chapel door.
And a hundred and twenty-seven saints whose bones
Are green grass in Killeaney
Will praise you with praises flashing on the eaves
Of heaven like wintry drops of rain.
But what of us, Padraic, what of us,
Men raised to the sea?

Poems of Maturity
(1946-1959)

Virgin

1.

The Lady who intervenes
In the Trinity assumes
Her rights on a side altar,
A great wick that no flame lames
In a quiet arch of candle flames.

And over the dim paving
Where drowned lights are stepping stones,
In the cave of the nave,
Soled with silence that stir like water
Or whispers of prayer the women falter.

Slowly, glimmering
One after one for a moment in that still arch
Each putting a penny in the money-box
Each lights a candle and burns there
As if she'd set it to her hair.

Then one after one each woman grows
Anonymous;
They pass and are the past;
O sighing history
Shuffling by that knee!

Candles will die for their small
Concepts of virginity but she
Older than the vine sits always in the sun
Turning on all the one face
Full of grace.

Moon to what sun?
Mother of one Son
Shall I turn my back upon you and walk out?
Ere I with women find you inside me –
A tree, a growing reverie?

A great reverie
Drinking a thousand roots in me,
Growing till it opens my skull, Who then
Will gather me up
When I flower at the top?

Her hands are not tangible;
Her face drifts; and over all
Her body is the quality of distance
And the shine of water.

If guesses were gods
How they would stride out towards her, seven leagues in
    each boot!
If gods are guesses, I am still moderate
In thinking they'd reach heaven through her thought.

How the heavens depend on her!
If her weather altered it would mean
Angels and their wide glories would drip from the air
Melting in a bright shower round her like rain.

How be intimate with this
Translucent Atlas? Yet sometimes I awake
Softly as if I had been kissed
And blessed, to feel the earth quake.

Farmer

Last winter a Snowman; and after snow an Iceman
Shattering, O cold, his bright blue limbs like glass
With ever frozen footstep; in the thaws that followed on,
A doll that almost melted into mud without a face.

What of it. The sun's in his hands now, hands of iron
That run too with the soft spark of clay,
His look is mild and large as the horizon,
He loses himself in the earth like a summer day.

But how he will come to you, woman, gathering up
His body in a thunder off the grass
In a four-legged gust, he's away and over the fields apace –
Tallyho, tallyho – with the whole wild earth at a gallop:
Just beckon, he'll roar up like weather, only to sway
So softly down you'll think him the month of May.

Assumption

Some Syrian rainmaker
Invoking a minor image of power found her
Intrude, O enormous magic, and his hands
Dissolve in showers over many lands;
Earth turned woman, or woman into earth, he
Left this wild image to Syrian sorcery.
But O how they tamed her, the Greeks, the civilising
Mythologising Alexandrian schoolmen
And the soft Italians with the Christian eyes
Who ferried her over the tideless Mediterranean;
The muted breasts, the quiet, and on the top
A face bright as a waterdrop.

Assumed into heaven, she,
A statue among statuary,
Consumes in her single fire the line
Of barbarous virgins who dwelt between
Trinities in their season.
Heaven and earth are in division;
The gross fertilities, the ram, the bull,
Left out-of-doors while in her shuttered parlour
When she bares the nipple
No rye rises, no wheaten flower;
Only her dreams stir
The peacock presences of air.

This mild lady
Calms the gross ambitions with a steady
Country look. No drums, no dances,
No midnight fires, no sacrifice of princes;
She takes her pail among the cows
And bolts her fowl in the fowl house;
Evoe, if the sun-headed god is gone, there's still
The house to be done, white linen hung
Upon the hedge. The serene axle
Goes round and round in a crucifixion
But earth is a pot of flowers. Foreign tongues
Commune above her in a drift of wings.

Poète Maudit

Mad as metaphor
You, Rimbaud, once. O petit amasseur des rentes,
When you buried the god did all the marvellous rant
Stop, or still seek in you the saviour?

You who were language to a field,
And a wood's identity walking, who felt silence
Turn its stones into birds when you were the all once
And worlds in words of glass revealed

Was there other sanity
After all that? Was he sane, the dead-eyed man
With the vision of a levelled gun
And all the inanity?

Adding all that never shows
Into a tradesman's ledger, the weeping nail-holes
In his hands, the unfeathered heels,
That forehead where a crown of thorns grows:

You who opened like a rose
Inside the very heart of contemplation
Where the poet oozes blood that's not his own
You, the flower and the cross,

The harmony of agony
And agony of harmony beyond thought:
Poet, when you buried the god, did Nothing still seek
        you out
In the night like sweat, a dark anxiety,

And maunder on and on
In its no-language, fumbling for the ghost
And the wild metaphor of the lost
And living god you buried under stone?

If Gods Happen

If Gods happen
Only when we throw our wild unreasonable
Desires into a kind of definition,
Are they us? and are we then illimitable?

And always journeying
Vastly through ourselves, with every start
A new discovery of that great thing
Inside the heart?

A god happening
When we have talked ourselves out of the little city
We have inhabited too long.
And space is our necessity?

Happening, yet old as if left over
From another world; when things finitely bid us
Be infinite, do we discover
In us or in a god the end of our neurosis?

For One is always there
As if a journey ended, and all longing
Had formulated Him, indefinite and clear
New, and oh the release, the self-delighting.

Our arrival towering
On the new beaches, old steeples and discontent
Lost, and our eternal talking
Drowned in the statement of a continent.

How large then this little beat
Of blood, this small dynastic pulse that throws
Such colonies out beyond all wit
And walls, this heart no taller than a rose?

The Mothers

The Mothers always know it for a lie.
Love me, they say, love me alone;
I am the mystery.
But having separated from her bone
We find the way of our new skeleton
Expanding towards the sky.
For every man is Adam and the tree
His own celestial geometry.

But the birth that divided us is always pain.
The wrench is there for gain or loss;
Two never one again;
For when the tree towers the God is jealous
And our myth always melting about us
Is so much rain,
Till something in the structure starts to give;
Our tall Euclid brings forth Eve.

Here's our second heart. And for all its loveliness
Flesh never learns the technique of persuasion;
A man is still a nakedness
Under his tree, and cold is the God's gaze on
The white fork where a rose marks the division:
O never again first Oneness.
Divided from it by the Mother's knee,
All poetry is our apology.

To the God the dignity; ours the shilling and the curse
And a heart divided in itself to mourn
Its own divorce;
Half-willing to be still a tower to heaven,
Half-willing to be the dark where love is given
Always for the worse:
A demi-god caught half-way up a cross;
And below, the woman who bemoans his loss.

J'accuse

These are curls on his head,
Not rings of mail, General. They will not save him
From gun butt or bayonet.
They please the eye and maybe someone's fingers.

That eager and innocent look
That meets you, General, is not armour-plated,
Not built, indeed, for the bullet
Issued today, you remember signing form this-and-that?

This perfect and gambolling body,
A marvel, General, eh? And well it might be,
Begotten as it was in love,
Alas, there is no bomb-shelter it can carry.

No place for my son safe,
No new planet, General, for you too would be there
To guard us early and late
From every possible and impossible invader.

And yet he will be killed, he is already dead,
General, of I know not what missile or poison. And his mother
Will not speak to me. Not a word is said
Between us two who were lover and lover.

Why does she accuse me,
General, with such white and disfigured silence? you
Will know surely, you can tell me.
You know such a lot you can tell me surely.

Is it because you had a father
Who didn't, General, strangle you at birth,
Or after, when you started playing soldier
On the table, before that table became the earth?

To One Newspaper Critic

The dog's problem is the tree:
The tree's problem never is the dog.
The tree has climbed so far away
It's lost in its own monologue.

It has climbed into its smoke,
And fixed it: from a seed no bigger
Than dog's droppings, it took one look
Then soared up to its proper figure.

And what is happening up there,
What major operation on the heights,
It tells no dog, though it must share
Its lower bark with him who bites.

Portrait of an Artist

The delicate head intent
On burning itself away escapes
Self-immolation by some miracle
Of modulation, stops
And makes such a lamp in what is relevant
This moment should be permanent:
Or else –

Else the world has lied
To her and made her up of themes
Not daily told and much too large for limbs;
And after she cried out,
Offered her this imago, monstrous skin,
Dilation; no other skeleton
But this –

Sweated and vapoury thing that grows
So bright in the negative, that is
The halo and the dedicated head;
Only she goes among the dead

Lighting her wisps, in words as bare
As nightlights trembling after her;
Leaving me –

Alone, boots, roots and all by the still canal
Of a moored morning stopped where a great swan
Has leaked fullgrown into his water-shade,
To find this face inside my head
Weeping for a girl known and gone
Away from me, though treetops in procession
Still follow me.

Yeats's Tower at Ballylee

Is every modern nation like the Tower
Half-dead at the top?
                                            W.B. Yeats

A pilgrimage is one slow foot
After the other, the agony of the heart
That looks to a place that will ripen like a fruit.
Yet I arrive in a Ford car
At the Tower talking of markets and wool
And corn drowned in the stook, the country around
Rain-rotten, the wet road buzzing like a spool
And trees at their year's end
Dropping the loaded sky to the ground.
I arrive talking of heifers and wool
And am confronted by the soul
Of a man in whom man cried like a great wound.

Somewhere a man will touch his image and burn
Like a candle before it. What happened here
In this ruined place of water and drowned corn
May still be here.
The oaken door hangs open, I go in
To a desolate underground that drips;
Shadows are on the stairs, the walls are weeping
A peacock paint, where a shoe slips
I clamber into a chamber like a tomb

Or a dim woodcut by William Morris
And suddenly I know the tower is
A boy's dream and the background of his rhyme.

Here where country blood was spilt
Neither earth nor stone cries out, for this is a dream-structure;
All that the brazen Norman built
To house a score of bullies in black armour
Deflected and turned to phantasy
By the boy who brooded on book and paint
Long mornings in his father's study
As medieval as a saint:
This is the Tower at last, its passion spent
And wearied of its own brutality
Where a boy could dream like Gabriel Rossetti;
Useless as verse and as magnificent.

I turn from the arty chimneypiece where glass
Has the pale wash of dreamy things and climb
Through a rude and navel arch, I pass
A sentry-go where no man turned a rhyme;
And the narrow stairway leads me to the place
Where he worked at the great table
Or lifted his tall height to pace
The enormous floor of his own fable;
Did he wear iron then, I wonder,
Or when the shadows stole the candle-light
Imagine himself all constellated night?
Il penseroso in the magic chamber?

Yet nothing is here but the wind in the swinging windows
And the roar of the flood waters far below
Not a house in sight, the corn in rows
Drowned and the drizzle rotting in the meadows:
The earth that cares for nothing but its seasons
Of lust and fruiting and death
Worked all about him here and gave no reasons
Why any man should waste his breath
In delicate definitions of a mild
World where man is the whole,
The individual soul
A heavenly cradle for the newborn child.

From the boy's dream to this reality
Of brutal weather and brutal stone
The Norman brought him. I come on the right day
To see for myself how earth can change a scene.
Rain and desolation, isolation
And fear in civil war can bring a man
To that harsh point in contemplation
Where soul no longer sees the sun:
In that bleak vision can man live,
Not summing up heaven and earth in measure?
Can he spend himself like a rich treasure
Where only the animal qualities survive?

Here at last he knew what opposites
War in one person. He became a man.
And the man divided into the primitive cross
Of two men in one rhythm. When the Norman
Came to the top the poet's words were blood
And what was good but a mere vision
Of arrogant foray, rape, and ride.
And then soul took its turn and with precision
Divined like an architect a house of life
Where violence had an energetic place
Only to find a holy face
Stare back serenely from the end of strife.

I climb to the wasting storey at the top.
His symbol's there where water and watery air
Soak through the plaster. The higher we clamber up
Into ourselves the greater seems the danger;
For the wider the vision then
On a desolate and more desolate world
Where the inspirations of men
Are taken by man and hurled
From shape into evil shape;
With the good and the grace gone out of them
Where indeed is there hope for men?
So every civilization tires at the top.

Around me now from this great height
Is a vision I did not seek. I have avoided it
And now I am forty-five
And wars blow up again, the east is lit,

Towns burn, villages are bombed,
With people everywhere in flight,
Their households on a handcart, or entombed
In homes that fell about them in the night
And dragging children homeless in the air;
A mass migration of the humble
Before some war-mad general.
O the higher we climb up the wider our despair.

This tower where the poet thought to play
Out some old romance to the end caught up
The dream and the dreamer in its brutal way
And the dream died here upon the crumbling top.
I know the terror of his vision now:
A poet dies in every poem, even
As blossom dies when fruit comes on the bough,
And world is endless time in which things happen
In endless repetition, every man
Repetitive as a pattern, no soul
But the sprawling spirit of the whole
Massing upon the careless earth like frogspawn.

Everywhere is the world. And not less here
Because the stream, dividing, moats the place.
To live a fairy tale he bought this tower
And married a woman with a pleasant face;
And built in bookshelves, cupboards, hung
His pictures up and walked around
His beehive and his acre, wrung
Some civilization from the ground:
And yet instead of rhyming country ease
As in the eighteenth century we find
Him raving like a man gone blind
At the bloody vision that usurped his eyes.

Below me in the road two countrymen
Are talking of cattle and the price of wool,
Glad of the gossip and something held in common.
That scene would have been peaceful
An hour ago, but now I stumble down
In horror, knowing that there is no way
Of protest left to poet or to clown
That will enlarge his future by one day.

I could beat a policeman, bawl in a square, do gaol
For something silly. And what avails it? I
Step into the drizzle of the sky
Despairingly, to talk of the price of wool.

Maris Stella

1.

In the flat glaze of the quays,
On stone where evening lies, the fishermen
Overhaul their gear.

And the light receives
Blue overalls and black rubber boots
And drowns them sometimes in a wintry flash
From which they recover themselves, fastened by the usual
    thoughts
To the bobbing floats of their familiar heads,
And find again their own appearances.

Around them always is the sea:
And inside them with no murmur over the ground
The sea; and below, how do I know
How many fathoms down
Their trailing limbs go?
Into what fishtailed memory?

Seas in their heads, too; do they turn
Over in their beds with every ebb and flood?
Their sleep wide-open weather
Where fish swim and birds cry
Over and around them and inside them forever?

So not as men only but living up and down
Their obscure spirals of air and water they
Add their little rhythms to the sea,
Each man an estuary.

Yes, almost unhumanly,
Almost finned and winged as fish and fowl,
Almost as certain as they
In their own elusive counterpoint they move out,
Not to collide with but to ride
All rhythms and forces
As centaurs, horses themselves, ride horses.

But so incessantly
Do they need to retrieve themselves from drowning
In boats, in thoughts, in seas outside and in, however,
They become aware, they know terror
As the other pulse, the greater.

And they dare not eavesdrop on themselves, they dare
Not look within where all the underworld
Is turning into myth
In lust and dream, in drama and terror,
All that they are
To utter you who are unutterable:
You, caught up like a breath,
The very last before death.

2.

Men with meanings
Inside that wait like cold wicks in oil,
Here they endure the wide stare of things
Roosting like seabirds, here they pull
Themselves out of the waters to keep station
On you like some continuous intimation:
Do you know them from other birds who fold their wings
Above the coasts and rain down droppings?

Are you always arriving ashore
And through them up some old waterstairs of feeling?
Are you the Igniter who climbs up the tower
Of their graze to light that archaic reeling
Lanthorn in each face?
Are you that cold thing in the gaze?
That barbarous look of the older climate
The halfmade man, the not-yet-private?

The fisheaters, the fishcatchers
Who rise arrayed in and shedding fishes like
Electric shocks, who disappear for days into the weathers
Of the Giant's house, but to ride
Out when all is lost to dodge upon
An immense and dangerous horizon
And only when we've lost all hope
Come home on a fair wind up the telescope?

Poem for my Mother

1.

That dismal country, Killimore-daly:
When my mother talks I know the place at once
And the faces of a century
All dead, but household gossip since;
And again she is my
Dream and my anatomy;
And my geography's that low blue knoll
Over the bog where the black miles are all
To the sky's far wall.

The first on her tongue is that gentle and precise
Grand-uncle James. He tilled the arable
And was a sacrifice
To ties I'd think intolerable.
He was a second son; and one night
When his elder brother's horse took fright,
The cart upturned, and with his brother dead
He found himself with a family ready-made;
And no woman in his bed.

A homely stately man, with an old oaken
Dignity and a courtly way of speech
That left unbroken
The delicate things in a child's reach:
To six girls he was
More than their looking-glass;

And I with my mother's eyes upon me see
The simple and major figure she'd wish on me,
The father I refuse to be.

James was a Dilleen. My mother's mother's people
Were the fair-haired Burkes from the bridge at Raford;
Millers whose old green wheel
Still grinds for a neighbour's board;
Beech and the bubbling poplar
Ride up the small trout-water
To the sheltered slates where once a harsh-faced wife,
Frank Burke's second woman, spent her life
And her good man's in strife.

A family legend, she; not kind it seems
To step-children. There was some whispered talk,
So my Grand-Uncle James,
The sturdy man, in his riding cloak
Rode out one winter night
To do the thing was right;
He downfaced the woman on her hearth, he took
The child from the coals and wrapped it in his cloak;
Her Lullaby his gentle look.

Pride of that night-ride's in my mother's eyes
When she talks of it. I hear the horse-hooves on
White frost, the stars and trees
Are Christmas; in the lamp six girls listen
And open the door to a call
To take a child like a doll
From an old man's arms – no, not a doll, a rose;
Rose of his heartbeat, as if his life's repose
Had flowered in his frozen clothes.

2.

But the woman of the mill, that temper on a hair
And the pride that's an appetite for self-destruction,
She's the one lays bare
The bones of chronicles: no ruction
But the terrible cerebral itch
Of a self-regarding bitch
Will not stir up, as if she found each place

Dull as a mirror, but in all wild displays
The life inside her face.

The Mill landlord was a jackboot in
The older style, but fair. He called one night
And asked Burke for possession
Of a park he'd leased. He'd all the right,
So Burke agreed. But the door
Opened and his wife with a glare
That silenced him, strode in convulsed and red
And threw a bag of sovereigns at his head:
Fight the bugger, she said.

Take this, the whole strongbox, and till it's spent
On law I'll never have enough of law,
Says she, O the termagant.
And law she had till out-at-elbow,
With Frank dead and the rent
Overdue, she went
Out of the chronicle to America;
Unmourned, unhonoured, even disliked in her day,
But a person in her own way.

She touched her time, but never the people; strange
For her quarrel was the quarrel of the time
When a land-squabble could arrange
Banners and processions and walk out in rhyme:
Does the country, in one who struts,
Guess the illness in the guts
Seeking a tall and suicidal end?
Whom the gods wish to destroy will find no friend
Where all are wise and bend.

3.

She was a figure of pride. There was another
Not far away, one of the quality;
And he, says my mother,
Had all the country's sympathy,
His name was Dominic John
Burke-Browne, a gentleman
Of blood so ancient it had lost the sting;
His home was a Norman keep, a naked thing;
The house a plastered wing.

Two sisters, spinsters, this proud bachelor had
With vague accomplishments. In rainy grandeur
One of the two went mad
And wandered the callows with goose and gander:
And when they'd drag her home,
Her neck stretched out in the spume
Of an angry goose, she'd hiss, they say. The other
Had buried her youth without much fuss or bother
And liked that Burke my grandmother:

So much that from the castle the soft fruit came
In baskets down the lane on summer days
From a Burke to a Burke, poor name
That used such different umbrellas;
And, gesture from kin to kin,
A man with a delicate cane
And the carpet walk of the sheltered bookman trod
The winter time up to his heels in mud
That the royal thing confer with its blood.

Old privilege, though he was a Catholic,
Had made it customary he should pray
Curtained away from Mick
And Pat on Sunday and Holyday;
But some Maynoothman with
No reverence for myth
Ruled that all men when down upon the knee
Before the Lord were the one family tree;
And took away his canopy.

He never passed the font again, they say:
And strangely no one blamed him. They had pity
For the proud old man on Sunday
For there in one high window he
Was seen to raise the glass
When bells rang out for Mass
And face the little chapel over the trees,
Missal in hand, upon his bended knees.
And no one felt at ease.

O the stories told about him. There were three
Fools in the parish, three old brothers who
Stole turf nightly;
And wondering if it were true
They were such fools, he set
A trap for them, he put
A crown-piece on a style between the quicks
They'd need to climb to play their usual tricks
On his Nobility's turfricks.

They came at dawn, sluggards, one, two, three
Homespun men, the eldest first as of right;
He passed unseeingly;
But the second saw it – and with no second sight:
Wondering, gibbering, he
Showed it and the three
Filled a pipe and passed it round and round.
To contemplate the better what they'd found,
They sat upon the ground.

A silver piece, and it could have been the moon
That had fallen down for all the complicated
Wonder it brought them. One
By one the younger were animated;
But the eldest, a man of laws,
Pondered all his saws
Till he found that which removed perplexity;
Says he, to each day that day's task, if it be
The turf today, then tomorrow we'll gather money.

The crown was returned to its place, the moon to the air,
And one by one they climbed in their innocence
A style and a townland's laughter.
But O Dominic, man of sense,
Were you the wiser, you
Who gave yourself to the blue
And bookish fiction and denied the red
Blood that clamoured for a girl in bed
And bedamned to the esquired dead?

What had you, O delicate hail-fellow to a book,
More than those slovenly louts who warmed their shins,
You, too, on the hook
Of a logical witless innocence,
You shown the chapel door
By a world you knew no more.
Your dispensation done, who yet strove still
To live your lie, who never lived your will,
Upon your purple hill?

4.

So much for Dominic Burke-Browne. He died
When my mother was young, and some herdsman moved in
And never, they say, thrived.
A place to end, not to begin;
An inimical place
To people born on the grass
Whose business is weather and the tillage patch,
All the simple traffic that needs no latch
Between fields and the thatch.

Ghosts, says my mother; and perhaps the dead can throw
Shadows sometimes that the living see.
One is a Dutchman who
Got the castle after Aughrim as his fee;
Not to enjoy it forever;
One night in an embrasure
When he struck a spark to light his pipe the wall
Glowed like a Dutch interior, and some tall
Burke blasted him with a musket ball.

She names ghosts one by one in her chronicle.
One story's funny. Three men sought shelter there;
Two were tall, so the middle
Of the bed was the small man's share;
All night his sleep was lost
For some Euclidean ghost
Whose delight was symmetry tugged till his feet lay
By the tall man's feet, then after some delay
Violently tugged the other way.

5.

Tale after tale she tells that brings me back
To a townland that's almost woman to me,
To the heart before the crack
To the peace before the poetry;
Back farther where the earth
Is my pre-natal birth,
Even beyond you, woman, who are tall
As the Mother of God, to your own watery knoll,
So blue where black miles are all.

Between Attymon and Cloonshicahill, between
Lisduff and Brackloon, Woman, O my maid,
In a townland never seen,
When all townlands were in your head,
You must have imagined a son
And he when your time was done
And it was his turn to seek your face inside
Discovered not a mother nor a bride
But a living countryside.

In all the levels of my eye you are;
And I divine you, I, your diving fork;
O my discovery of water,
You always here where poems work.
No dwindling woman with
A worn face but the myth
That magnifies, hurts, and satisfies till all
My gaze is gathered up upon the tall
Mountain where Muses dwell.

Be there away, but mostly here beside
My blood, in the humdrum of your chair, be you
Most plainly and abide
As if the fire and lamplight too
Found you a resting place;
Mistress of my house, and let this room be kind
From gazing on you when I draw the blind
On the night outside my mind.

Pot Shot

I tell words that talk in trees, this hill
Is my vocabulary, and when I lie down
The sky seizes me so very quietly
I reflect the sunset, the river and I are one.
And then the gun goes off. Am I that, too?
Thunder and blast? And when the hooves of the echoes
Have galloped over the grass and the field aloofly
Returns to itself and silence on its toes
Cranes to hear a rabbit squeal, am I
The wound that I give, the hurt I hurt, the shiver
That talks so tall in trees, that is the sky,
That explodes in death, yet walks like the wide river
So calmly through the evening that I tame
The world around me till it names my name.

Vowels

A: Watermaid, the frantic virgin who
Yet hides her birth where man must hatch it. E:
Distant and elongated drapery,
The lady-never-won whom all men woo.
O: midsummer woman, countryside
And sway, the opulent bed, the wed, the bride.
U: is my mother gathering up the view,
Majestic, with an apple on her knee.

But I: I, is my danger; my knotted thread
And needle's eye; my ancient grandmother
Who tells my follies while she sews my shroud.
At times she fades as if not made of matter,
And then again her glance is all a glitter
When she lifts her shears and chatters with the dead.

Dialogue between Raftery and Death

Argument: Raftery the poet finds that his mistress, a married woman, is having an affair with a visiting sailor. The shock is severe and he considers death for the first time as a part of life. Tradition tells us that he saw the bony figure of death one night in his room; and that he who was blind found his sight while the vision lasted. He denied this vision later, however, under pressure from the clergy, and I prefer to take it as I write it here.

RAFTERY: There is someone here?

DEATH: Yes, Raftery.

RAFTERY: I know the voice

DEATH: You know the voice.

RAFTERY: I do. It walks on all my drums. It fills me
Fuller than my heart. I have such noise
Inside me that the red rope of my pulse
Rocks me like a bell-tower. Visitor,
Are you inside or outside all my walls?
Are you Raftery's angel, that wild trumpeter?

DEATH: No, Raftery. Never a trumpeter.

RAFTERY: Who, then?

DEATH: A Dignity that lacked a voice till this,
And so long silent, you may call me Silence.

RAFTERY: You use an alias so, for Silence is
The nightly gift this room gives Raftery.
You have another name?
        I need not delve.
The steepletops are still, yet toll it slowly
And all the clocks strike twelve.

You are an angel of death?

DEATH: Yes, Raftery.

RAFTERY: A moment ago and I was throwing myself
From every tower. Now strangely I find dignity
Inside me once again.

DEATH: O, at the end it's natural
For death to be received so quietly.

I am so quiet myself, indeed, I invoke
Quiet so palpable I leave it after me
As you might leave the scent of tobacco smoke
And, by the by, you smoke too much.

Raftery looks up for the first time

RAFTERY: And you
         Are death?

DEATH: Just your particular death.

RAFTERY: I'm honoured, by God.
         I have a death the spit of Loss the grocer

DEATH: Now, more respect –

RAFTERY: O, all the pipes aboard
         Will shrill for the admiral. But I'll have a death that look
         Like Death and not like poor meek Loss, whose sister
         Kept him collecting jumble clothes for blacks
         Till he, too, went in dread of the human figure.

DEATH: I am what you have let me be. I, Death, am
       The twin of Life, you know. With you we knit
       In one and make you a person. And a nasty time
       I've had of it, my twin your favourite
       From the very first, never a thought for me;
       Always ignored. And the house never quiet.
       You two jaunting, drinking, bringing women home
       And singing, dancing, raving, ranting; every night
       Bright as a brothel; no thought for a nice quiet tomb.

RAFTERY: I do not believe it.

DEATH: What?

RAFTERY: That you are Death.

DEATH: I insist that you believe in me, Raftery. You must
       Allow me at least the dignity of existence.

RAFTERY: Death imposes more. The Striker. What!
              And the Strider of our dust.
         The lightning flash, the thunder on the house.

DEATH: But I am – I mean I would be – I believe
              I could be
       Thoroughly terrifying . . .

RAFTERY: Maybe to a mouse . . .

DEATH: But you ignore me, and give me no chance, Raftery.
I've lived like a prisoner – no, an exiled Royalty –
Inside you, Raftery; downcast, downtrodden because
You would not even become aware of me;
Why, tonight's the first time you have loaned me a face
And what a face. Other men's deaths can wear
The loveliest frightful masks, but I have this
Parody as if you'd kicked my rear.
You are no gentleman, then a poet never is.
O, I was born unlucky. Give me a king
And I could be so vast and royal a shiver
All lamps would seek me out. A throne's the thing
For ghostly eminence. You've heard of Alexander
But never how night uncrowned him, how that
    Conqueror
Who'd so much sun he'd scorch a neighbouring
    hamlet
Was after dark but a star-and-gartered nightmare
All the great Asian gutters running sweat.

RAFTERY: You do not listen?
Vanish, now, you interrupt me.

DEATH: But you called me.

RAFTERY: When?

DEATH: You wished to die.

RAFTERY: And God's grey footman ran obediently?
Is a lover allowed no rhetoric? What if I did cry?

DEATH: Must I leave emptyhanded?

RAFTERY: Take me then. Or try.

DEATH: You hold the ground
Like a stone monument.

RAFTERY: Do I hear you sigh?

DEATH: I cannot move you.

RAFTERY: Vanish then, or not a sound.
You interrupt my quarrel with the sky.

DEATH: Another squabble with God? The old story
Of your soul, that trouble-the-house. If you had not a
soul,
You'd still invent one, Raftery.

RAFTERY: Never. The soul ignites me
Like a spill of paper. Who'd be the fuel
Of a sky-climber only to go on fire?
Soul burns everything, every love, it serves
My body worse than a syphilitic father,
A lunatic runs up and down my nerves.

Can't I love without soul?

DEATH: Love. Love. Is the life principle
One vast erection, a candle in a windy cave?
You do not need this flary fellow ....

RAFTERY: It is not sensible
To burn like this. Every woman's a grave,
And a corpse is all love needs. Yet Raftery
Is wrung by some tall lunar thing, wings beat
In heaven when he loves. O, Raftery
Has too much of God for two clay feet.

I put the case to heaven. A man should walk
Untouched from woman to woman and take his
pleasure.
My text is lechery ...

DEATH: Jack Soul up his beanstalk,
God's glittering gossip ...

RAFTERY: Every woman's a whore,
And lust is enough, for the pain when it aspires ...
Distraction of moonlight, the donkey gallops around,
He brays from the grass, white rage to his flattened
ears
But the moon's no mare to be covered from the
ground.

DEATH: You've taken up my theme and now you speak
My life aloud. I'm the tired flesh inside
Already muttering because trumpets break
The lovely silence. The Soul will sound for pride,
Go chiding, striding, in all its ignorance

That we who're not combustible can tire
Of wings and things and only ask the silence
That lets us fall asleep about the fire.

RAFTERY: You are here still?

DEATH: Why, I'm stronger, now.
Your flesh argues for me.

RAFTERY: Don't you know yet
That every love invents me all anew?

DEATH: Nonsense. Your dreams unbuild you every night.
You know you've too much wisdom to go on
Enforcing Soul on the body, accumulating guilts
For nothing. Why, even if you love this woman,
She's only your death-wish walking round on stilts.

I undermine you a little?

RAFTERY: I see you'll try
Another tilt in a minute.

DEATH: I'm trying now,

RAFTERY: I scarcely notice.

DEATH: Raftery, that is a lie.

RAFTERY: A little lie, perhaps. You've found some power
You didn't have at first. It's not enough.

DEATH: But you're aware of me.

RAFTERY: I know you're here.

DEATH: The first black shadow. It's a curious stuff
That tailors itself; it's Life's black underwear.

I chill you a little?

RAFTERY: I stoke the fire
Just that little more. Do you go away?

DEATH: I stay, of course. Your Great Corrupter.
From this time on I lend you my strange eye.
A vision of acid, Raftery. You look upon
A face and the face turns blank, the marvellous living
Mask collapses on the skeleton
Before your eyes; and behind it – only nothing.

59

RAFTERY: Against that nothing, I can think of a face
            That startles me, a woman's face that floods
            My whole house with sun and tall stained glass . . .

DEATH: Against that nothing those few coloured muds
            Are less than nothing. And the moody woman within
            Already knows the hands of a certain tailor
            And the garment he tailors, so she lives in sin
            And tries to forget him with a common sailor.
            But you know all this.

RAFTERY: I know it, O God.

DEATH: And still you live. And the sailor is still alive.
            For all your poetry and frenzy, poet,
            The seaman's got her. And still he is alive.
            How the Liberties will mock you over the case.
            Mock you more than that poor man, her husband;
            The poet cast for a jockey of the high seas,
            A high-rigged boy with a bellyfull of wind.

RAFTERY: I have no hangman's taste for certain neckwear.

DEATH: A lovely instrument. One string finds all
            Silence in a note; an instrument for a lover
            Since all great love is suicidal.
            If you love greatly, then leave your love behind
            Fixed like a stone, your wildness in a gesture;
            Arrange it, Raftery, be forever self-contained;
            Death is the measure of a lover's stature.
            And the peace after the glory. To leave behind
            A self in people's minds . . .

RAFTERY: The glory is the slut's
            Who could excite such passion, and for the suicide
            Peace is a burial with a stake down through his guts.

DEATH: But someone must die for love. It should be you
            Who love love loudest.

RAFTERY: To sing love is my trade.
            I'll go on singing if only to prove to you
            A living poet is better than a dead.

            I see you no longer.

DEATH: (faint)	Do you mean, I can't be seen?
RAFTERY:	You've gone.
DEATH:	I'm here, I'm here.
RAFTERY:	And scarcely to be heard. Have I finished you?
DEATH:	No. I'll be strong quite soon.
RAFTERY:	Soon enough, when I'm whiskered and grey-haired, A crutch in my hand and the priest beside my bed And no tall woman smiles at me from a poem. Where are you now?
DEATH:	I think I'm – once more dead.
RAFTERY:	Then let us call a general post-mortem.

Maud Gonne

Somewhere in this city
She must have left herself, somewhere
Left her heartbeat
In one tall rose of space;

Left herself, the whole
Body and glitter in a moment, like a niche,
Fixed there, gesture and all,
But living, living through every fingertip.

The passion still
A well, a vowel; through a lover or a thought
She streams in an endless jet against the will
Of time. I look for that wild silhouette

And bless the south and north and east,
The west where I was born I bless
That four impersonal mirrors may throw back at me
The sea-cold currents of her face.

61

2.

Gods are our journey into space;
But here, if passion were high, a single flower
Offered to her might shake the place
With so much life your flower could disappear,

Yes, flowers could be taken from my hands and my hands talk
Back to me from wonder and miracle,
The space between hands and heart so tall with shock
Fingers scarcely know the girl.

Gods who transform the simple touch
Of lust are kind. O, out of the blue damps
Of Ireland this great ache in me must read
A face that will burn all my lamps.

She will be helmeted, outrunning her own hair
Serenely, winged with a large look.
Ah Christ, if one could scrape off time like paint
And for once just be moonstruck.

3.

Trees and lawns at the windows.
An armchair. The fitful sleep. The tall clock ominous.
This is an old woman full of shadows
Returning to her eyes, who slowly becomes luminous.

This is the last of her, a still
Gaunt lamp of a woman with a wasting wick.
How calm is the face that burns the precious oil.
But I call on the girl within, I beckon the first face back.

And I think surely as I enter the courtyard
Of that large look and its paving of light, I need
Only a trumpet and the horned gate, Omega,
Would open wide to Alpha, the tall, the white-kneed.

I drop roses on the folded hands
And time receives them. O, let them fall far back
At the girl's feet where, stripped and full of fury,
She rages to scatter herself along the track.

The sculptors gather round her, the sculptors show
As she moves out of their hands into clay and bronze
Her public face of ravage and shadow,
A gaze that drops tears like stones.

A woman with a heavy reverie
Of tired eyes and the large loafing calms
Of age, a woman worn as history
With the world's lost causes pleading from her palms.

All the tired flourish ending in this stone
In a public square. That's what the woman in her
Who hated the woman wanted, it was her ambition;
And she has a kind of public life forever.

But O the revenge when the hands begin to dream
Of lovers she dented, the long dead,
And she cannot think for stone and the stars and the traffic stream
And the gulls that foul her head.

Leave her to us, the poets. We will make her
Litanies, and give our furies
A fulcrum that will lift and spread around her
Feelings like new territories,

This woman who knows no gravity
That waterfalls down the spine is not for you.
She is our story.
The sudden lifting of the brow.

She who inhabits a great lens
Like vision, who increases all our themes
Has left you nothing that can be touched with fingers
But something tall still walks into our poems.

And we fade through the lonely and passing phases of flesh,
And a silence sings. O tall moon on the hill
Mother of trees and their slow striding,
Mother of towers that stand still.

And yet to create a way
Of words where she may walk into a poem
Is to deceive you, my heart, O red giant inside me.
Life, not death, should be our theme.

If rooms still beat like hearts, if silk speaks to me strangely
In the language of a body, it is one we cannot touch.
That way lies futility,
Better the tribal bitch.

Better the woman who loosens your great knots
Of muscle, giant, in all the hates of love.
Do not listen to the poets.
Love is only to be alive.

Love will sell you out. But even so you will
Still have your nature left for that last aloof
Moment when you leave the millwheel.
Enough, Samson, to shake down the roof.

Love Poem

It was not difficult for Blake: they gossiped
Daily, reality and he. But I,
A poet, too,
Find it the bodily thing outside the body,
Yet near it, like a wound upon the thigh.
And so I seek you
Like pain; and when like pain you've slipped
Over my borders again, there's still this lack.
Heaven's up a strut and I'm no steeplejack.

And where's the communion? You with a tailored God
Neatly made to measure, who will sit
Inside and share
A woman's world all day and talk of it:
And yet with a look the whole tall stick is lit

And your head of hair
Becomes an adventure far above your head.
I know it, I, who never walked down the street
Like Blake, but took a cushion to your feet.

Book of Job

The simple thing is to die
So often and so painfully that I
One day in one breath
May live the whole life of death.

The daily thing is to be
Defeated daily, that this psychology
Of victory be unlearned
And sham into shame be turned.

For this Image is not Me;
This worldling satisfied and stately, with his family
Thanksgiving, and each day success,
The world always answering yes.

In this gift of luck I have lost
The naked traffic of the ghost
Trapped in an image I projected
Not of God but God's elected.

So the next thing is to ride
Horse and all under and be no more a pride;
No, nor an humility,
For that's a pride too, on one knee.

But to be nothing till
Flesh fall off and my heartbeat sounds real;
Until my heart is heard
Stammering with excitement its one word.

Come then rags and plagues
I am honoured to lend you my legs;
Enter this suffering house
Where honours fall off, where I delouse,

And bless me no more, You
In the twittering evening: O tall fall of dew
You fathered me so much ease
I ponder all misery now to find my peace:

I have my occupation; I will die
Into nothing after nothing, but live no lie,
Stripped to a faint shiver, waiting here
On a faint illumination in the air.

A Flask of Brandy

You, said the Lionwoman,
Pliz, this errand, a snipe of brandy
From the first shop. Here's money;
And for you this penny.

And on my way I saw:
Item, a clown who waltzed on stilts;
A bear saluting with a paw;
Two pairs of dancing dogs in kilts;
Eight midget ponies in a single file,
A very piccolo of ponies;
Then the princess far off in her smile;
And the seven beautiful distant ladies:
And then –

Facing after the big bandwaggon, he
The boy in spangles, lonely and profound:
Behind him the Ringmaster, a redfaced man,
Followed by silence heavy as a wound,
And empty.

Quickly as two feet can did I come back
To the Lionwoman with her cognac.

You, said the Lionwoman;
Pliz to the window, said foreign gutterals in
The cave of the caravan.
I waited, errand done.

And waiting on one foot saw:
Item: a twitching coloured chintz
Moved by a lemontaloned claw:
And after a woman with her face in paints,
A throat thickened in its round of tan
On shoulders sick and white with nature;
Behind was a pair of bloomers on a line,
Blue; a table with a tin platter:
More else:

A black electric cat, a stove, a pot
Purring, and a wild Red Indian blanket
Crouching sidewise on a bunk;
And some exciting smell that stunk
Till the Lionwoman rising blotted out
All but a breast as heavy as a sigh
That stared at me from one bruised eye.

The Head

1.

The day after decapitation
Was no wound yet. Noon found the head
Excited still and still singing
The visionary woman, still exalting
The woman in measures to which no words came
Off the black tongue. The river flies
Were busy on specks of blood, in clouds upon the hair;
But where her praise was fixed upon his face
No one had died, the flesh was adequate;
And on a mouth that seemed alive
Only the smile was anti-clockwise;
But no wound yet.

That night it drifted on
Through stars that buzzed no brighter, inches
Of radiance before it and around
That felt no wound;
And this was dyed with a flutter of vague moths,

And overhead where a curious white owl
Dilated, there was some reflection too;
And down below
More of it and stranger, for the eels
Had scented blood and wavered under the wicker;
This was a head that trickled down many tails
Into the deeps, eddying without end;
And still was felt no wound.

The slow morning came
Back to the eyes and brought the labouring crow
(Corvus corax corax) who discharged himself
Upon the skull unskilfully and cawed
Once, twice, and there for long was still.
The gulls disturbed him when the eyes were gone
And over the bloody mess rose such confusion
Three salmon fishers rowed out from a draft
Only to retch their morning stirabout:
That noon the skull gaped
And still was felt no wound.

The second afternoon it rained;

Rinsing the ruin the nozzled drops removed
Sundry strips, tissues, barber's clippings
Odds of nerves, bits, leaving such scrags, jags
And rags as still clung and dripped
To shine strangely when the sun came out.
The waters steamed a little before night
And from the skull where little pools remained
There oozed a smoke, a vagrant and hairlike smoke;
And in the hollow eyes the rain
Was bright as sight, and so it seemed
The nose put forth its bridge again,
And from the earholes arched two tufts of fawn
Two gilded wisps, the ears. The face had dreamed
Itself right back again.
And still no pain;
Still the exultant thing was fixed, and dawn
Found the bare teeth beautiful.

2.

The third day repeated as before
Washed out the skullhouse and refurnished it
With the changeable midsummer weather:
The head alone at last
Was bonebare and beaming; and where it floated
Down the broad vowel of the river, once
Its song was heard;

Snatches only, faint upon the ripple
And weirs of the water-word: a thin
Piping.

The reeds heavytopped tipped to it
As to a breeze.

          So it was the wind
That used the tattered wizen of the throat
As well as the sockets of the eyes, the earholes
And the pit behind the nose for hollow music,
Not overlooking the jewels of the mouth
That still smiled
For yet no wound was felt.

So time stopped
Outwardly, but there was still this woman
In the weather of the head
Who was all time to it no longer human.
And in that time the head came

By stages of water world
From green granaries, tilled, from fat uddered
Cow-lawns by river houses, woods that spoke in oak
And heavy roots and clumped along the banks
To a country narrow low and cold
And very thin like a wire,
Where the head sang all day.

There the seas fell inland almost vacantly
Over a sieve of sand;
There the head lay

While the coracle under it of sally withes
Dried, withered in sunlight, salt sealight,
Rotted till the ashen thwart that held the head
Rigid and singing, sprung the spent lashings,
Tipping over;
This, one day when the set from the southwest
Piled up an equinoctial on the coast;
On the white shore with no one to notice
The head fell.

And broke

In a separation of its major and distinct parts.
Two.

And from the still centre where was the true
Bubble or heartbeat, came the tiny whimper
Of some unhouselled thing;
The head's first cry
At last and never heard

By gull, gale, sandpiping bird
Or gannet in the tall and touselled blue,
Nor the wader on two pins nearby,
Though the cry was human,
The pain spreading greatly, going
Towards blood in every direction

But never arriving
Near and away where the woman was
Doing the usual things to men and clothes
Afraid of the glass,
Groundswell and undertows,
What happens and the happening
That will never come to pass.

Women

1.

The pity of it. Not to love
All the love we lean upon;
Always to be at some remove,
Always to be drawn
Towards the overwhelming one
We must meet alone.

O loneliness. We are born to them:
As mothers they mother us;
We break the navel cord like a limb
That as lovers they may love us:
But recover us
And leave them for our loneliness.

2.

Rest, says the earth. And a woman delicately
Says 'It is here, it is in my arms somewhere'
But a woman is a lie
And I have a tower to climb, the tower of me,
And a quarrel to settle with the sky
But 'rest' says the woman. 'O lean back more:
I am a wife and a mother's knee,
I am the end of every tower.'

Coastal Waters

Holy Well

In the annals saints
Sit in holy wells, talk freely
To grim hermits, heal
Who ails, the foot-holy
Pilgrims who walk in wishes.

The dumb speak, the cripple
Walks, the blind
Find the dazzling world of the mind
In new pigments. Here
The ways of God seem wayward but very clear.

Speak the word, Saint,
In your welling mineral
That world in a bright and single jet
Go up, and inside it, lit up,
God my space and my material.

The Dwelling

At night the house grows
Around the blackshawled woman. Harsh
And sparse the bony room
But with the lamp
All the pieces give their lights:
She shines among her satellites.

Man-chairs of oak, scrubbed; a rack
Of cups and blue plates;
The tabled jug:
The oilcloth spreading from the wick;
The spindled stair without a rug
But scrubbed, scrubbed to the quick.

The tiny window's shut its eye;
Let the strand roar
And the white horses tumble on the shore,
Here catgreen
The salt driftwood purrs inside the fire
And the sea ends that pours around the world.

Somewhere an old working clock,
Weights and chains, ticks on and tells
The woman's hours;
The wether's wool in the knitted sock,
The world weather in
Her knotted face, her knotted talk;

How men come home
From the ocean drip, still rocking, ill at ease
Till she gathers them;
Here she sets them down in peace
Inside the lamp, the house, the shawl.
Here is the centre of them all.

And all the pieces hang
In one. The man is on the chair
Who winds the clock
Who'll climb the stairhead after her,
Adjust the wick
Till the great night idles, barely ticking over.

Day Ashore

Sundays the long boat of the week
Is drawn up, turned keel over on the sand;
Rest, fellows, on the old
Wall, bellying the wind.

Here the sea colour shoals
And the Pole fails to pull. Rest, fellows,
On your rock pillows
And the small seas that sleep in shells.

Tomorrow the heave as earth turns over
Into Monday. Take your ease.
Light the pipe. Sit on forever.
Forget you're cold saltwater to the knees.

Tradesmen's Entrance

Love

1.

The strong man
Is he only after all the creature of what seems
Desirable, whom nothing else can
Please because once it was all the boy's dreams?

A girl on a horse
In the leaves of autumn, in the careless havoc of the air;
Behind her over the lawn the big house,
And she prouder for that house there.

Magnificent the dream
To the boy who peers from the wall. She gallops on
But never away, the house there all the time,
Skies unmoving, the journey never done.

2.

Ring out
Bells, give the lads a holiday;
Shutters down and shops shut, a stout
In every fist. It's love will find a way.

Love, or its dunce
The desperation that throws in its hand
Before the miracle happens that for the nonce
Will open up the land.

Is it always she,
The first, the almost forgotten, some ancient lie
That shattered us with truth, who is the enemy
And must be triumphed over for the boy?

Bless them. Ring, Bells.
They are what they are, they have what they have, enough
For whom the bell tolls
To tell their desperate stuff.

Peasantry

In a thatch
That could be a stable but for the open hearth
A man is born, the tiller of the earth.
Labour there, dumb brothers,
And have no wild itch
To raise yourselves. The world is to your betters.

In the mall,
Discreetly behind curtains, servants wait
On money that makes itself early and late;
And with the cash goes credit
And breeding, all
Ripening of the person. This the rich inherit.

Walk the town,
Tiller, interloper, up and down, we
Who live upon you will allow this free,
But close our heavy doors
To any clown
Born to the thatch in the boor-stink of the byres.

First Love

And so it arrives, the moment
Of moments; not much to it, yet.
A pale pigtail of a moment,
The look not even languorous, nor the poise
Very delicate:
Little to indicate the torment
To come, or the woman in the girl's disguise;
A moment, even, that a boy can forget
And if he does remember it
Will find it is the stir in every story;
As if the Goddess, in a shiver from the sea
With her birth-bud trailing, but tall in a fleeting wet
Uncertain glory,
Made all his memory her mythology.

And already they are enemies;
Each seeking the thing not to be had,
A mirror for the eyes
And the larger equation of the self that is
Not balanced in a bed;
Nothing here to indicate the sighs
To come or tell them that whether they kiss
Or do not kiss the heart and head
Start their journey to the dead.
The thing she will remember will not vex
Her housekeeping, but he stands where the decks
Are stacked. Be careful of this equation, lad;
Unbalanced X
In all its powers is another sex.

The Poems of Love

All the poems of love are one;
All women too. The name that runs
Profanely between love and lover
Is the name repeated over
In the rosaries of nuns.
All the poems of love are one.

Solar red, masochist black,
There's precedent for each in heaven;
Whatever be a body's leaven
The rosaries of the holy nation
Thrill to some transfiguration.
Love makes up the thing we lack.

All the women Tom and Jack
Buy or bed, the slumtown tits,
Have bright otherworld habits;
A queen shares pillows with a clown,
Still nebulously wears her crown,
And is most royal on her back.

When Tom and his hedge mistress come
Drunken to the judgement seat,
The obscene measures on his tongue
Start the heavens into song;
Endlessly must Tom recite
The love he made by rule of thumb.

And brawling face and bawling gums
Fade fawnlike into some young grace;
Love lives serenely many ways;
Love lives in all that it may not lack
Its body in riots, drunks and drums
And the rosaries of nuns in black.

The Animate

Her mirror told her once it was
A mistake not to be beautiful:
And something ebbed away from her.
But as her face diminishes
And almost as flesh vanishes,
Nerve living on nerve until
I can see her naked will,
Her intense skeleton discloses
The most unaccountable of roses.

On this top rock a wintry and rough
Wide plaque of sea-sky does not dull
Your delicate and deliberate reds:
You know that life is to the tough
And that your inches are enough
To show what is incalculable –
Love that makes the mirror tall
And gives you the image that you sought,
Thighs that tower beyond thought.

Orestes

Black oracles
That bid the tall son slay the mother
Follow on the heels
Of the lover
Coming to take him over.

Purgation past,
The fiddles play the young bride from behind
Curtain and ghost.
Is the bridegroom blind?
The son out of his mind?

This is vengeance
Outside all sense, beyond all reason
And resonance;
Mother and son
To marry so and be one.

Odysseus

Last year's decencies
Are the rags and reach-me-downs he'll wear forever,
Knowing one day he'll sober up inside them
Safe in wind and wife and limb,
Respected, of unimpeachable behaviour.

Meanwhile he goes forward
Magniloquently to himself; and, the fit on him,
Pushes his painful hobble to a dance,
Exposing in obscene wounds and dilapidation
The naked metre of the man.

His dog will die at sight of him,
His son want fool-proof, and his lady-wife
Deny his fingerprints; but he
With his talent for rehabilitation
Will be his own man soon, without ecstasy.

Evening Off

Naked down to the maker's name
Warranted, nubile,
The well-women, the famous Nine in their dance,
Have nothing on this girl in appearance:
They the lovely words of mouth;
She the bubble of dense youth.

For the rest, they drive;
And she, the driven,
Knows the new coat she wears is not her own
Opinion of herself, she put it on
As something that might happen her
With these, the high tight shoes that hurt her.

Ladies, you, too,
Sometime did likewise:
Or your heavy mothers, fresh from outfarms, did;
Go easy with tongue and stare, she does but add
Something from her own rainbow
To what she sees in the shop window.

And if she offends –
Leading round as she does
Her afternoon off, like a cow with one horn
She cannot park, it is difficult to be born;
Yourselves know that journey
From nothing to identity.

Leave ill to the witch-face
Watching her from the lane-mouth;
This girl's time will come, the illtime; now the bells say
Sweet high-up and distant: 'Dear Dulcibella!'
The great belly will come
But now she wears her latest letter home.

Purely she tells
Herself from those heel-stilts
That wobble to mother, father; and still she sees
That boy at the corner straighten up his knees:
Speak, Ladies, tell how
Everything, anything, happens to her now.

Tell her this knobbly young
Hairslick with the fag end on his tongue
Unfolding from his corner in a look
So townwise will be all her luck and crook:
Time strung like a guitar
The dear bells so sweet and far.

Totem

They knew it, the Totem people, the world
Inside the world where man
Makes metaphors
For the animal.

And all this day it intrudes, static
Of older inhabitants, saurian, aborted wing, flipper, fur,
And the wavelengths thereof
Babbling of a broken covenant

Because an old sick cow was put down;
Murder, they say: as if blood shed
From sheer pity dyed
The ghost red,

Set horns tangling in the thicket
And heaven to collapse, as it must
To every act of treachery, in
A jangle of broken trust,

Our mutual world
Impossible with images
Of pain; today
An old lady bled herself away

In Flatfield on the headland; into
October she went, the day lying
To its grass anchors
In autumn scent.

Plumbing her mound soon will be briar and berry;
Deathbed for a Muse.
A post mortem to go on
Forever in the dogrose

Wherein this old shambling skeleton in rawhide
Is totally translated and taken over:
Here in a way lies
Everybody's mother

Confusing certain formal issues, an
Ambiguous body at best, straddling
Source and origin like
The first dolmen,

Requiring the old almost religious
Liaison, from whose
Mysterious totem bones I must ask pardon
For a pact broken

Thus acknowledging the ancient status
Of a quite ordinary creature who yesterday
Was horns not halo, whom heifers
Followed, whom we put down

By the haw hedge, cress and water near
And the orchard
That tells the weather to the falling apple
And rounds the echo travelling towards Tuskar.

Meeting

Countryman, consumptive;
Some children, four, I believe;
Now burned by a sun of another colour,
Tells me again good-morning – sir.
This is truth, too, in one posture.

And easily related
To something already much stated
But always forgotten till a feeling thinks for me
The moment-to-moment philosophy
Of my overpressed mortality.

It does not moralize,
This feeling, but accepts that a man dies,
Daily and wearily; the portents are too plain,
Time running out through every vein,
The face the terminus of pain;

Continuously arriving there
Without shock and secretly, but almost bare
And terrified already. I could stand
And talk of seasons and the land,
But he'd see through me and understand.

And hear under my breath
Words that condole with my own death
That seems so distant now, and me too
Sounding the bull-head of my strength, anew:
Spitting where he must swallow down the chew.

Field Observation

There died last night
In a poor thatch that whiskered heavy man
Who used to go my road
Peaceful as Saturn and as countrified;

In a flit of moonlight,
With the town dwarf complaining in his sleep,
He left corpse and corner,
A broken pot and one bright glass of water.

No more will all things cast
His measure, horoscope or the great size of his breath,
Who was each year reborn
In the annual excursion of the corn;

Who moved in the gravity
Of some big sign, and slowly on the plough
Came out anew in orbit
With birds and seasons circling him by habit;

Morning fell upon
His horses, and the weather moved behind;
From cold Christmas he
Moved up the hill in every leafing tree.

Now the windy fallow
For harmony must invent him in its turn
Whiskers, seeds and eyes,
His bags about him and his flapping skies;

One day the low-fired sun
In hedges bare and barbed as rolls of wire,
An old stiff half-rayed figure, the sole reason
For each divulging season;

In hayloads lost in June, in
Autumn the wheaten man, while
At their harps together
His strawpale daughters tinkle in the weather;

No other kin, not one
Beam from the blues in the cold cowyards round
The mountain where the crows knew him but never
The women clinging to the winter flaws;

And leaves no name
A season won't erase, old Walrus-face
Who lined the surging team
On a long furrow straight as the morning beam.

Johnstown Castle

1.

The summer woods refuse to meet
Us on the levels we know. We have evolved
Too much mind for them, and picked up feet
That solve things differently, like birds:
Trees use the old vocabulary
In all its ponderous gravity;
We with inner needs to be resolved
Have learned all the new and air-borne words.

Why intrude here, and why regret
An old root that like a rocket goes
On exploding season after season
In the same galaxy of leaf, without a reason?
All it knows
Is the old wholesome suit of clothes:
Never the new and complicated rose.

2.

An ornamental water
Should be backed with mercury that the sculptured swan
May be ideal swan forever.
Here one shiver shows the mud
And I am glad because a swan
Can turn up his end and shatter mood
And shatter mirror,
Till the woods massed in an architecture shake
Because a real swan mucks up a lake.

An old lady, slender as her wand
Of ebony, and carrying her castle still about her,
Is near me anywhere I stand;
My own creation.
I give her words to say, and a world, too,
Homelier, perhaps, than that she knew,
And take an interest in the conversation:
But as I ramble on
Creating all for her
I think how certainly she lived this view

84

Merely by walking over the ground
Day after day; I falter
For now my words take on another hue
And such a sound
I'm half afraid to turn around.

3.

Always my own monologue
Intrudes; things work into the word
Only to be imprisoned, or kennelled like a dog;
So the tall pine describes
A straight line up to the tuft of foliage
That sits it like a bird
And is only so much language
Because I use the word;
And all the ponderous oaks and the ooze underfoot,
All the harsh nerves of an old wood
That are a rumble in the nether-gut,
Are not what one transcribes
And never any good;
The monologue intrudes, my words let me
Into a poem, not into the poetry.

And yet a man must walk
Out of his mystery, if he's to meet it
Face to face, in talk,
And guess from words omitted the major and delicate
Evasions of his ghost
Who is the host
To every massive feeling and must live it.
Create me, says the poet, I am a body
For every word, the large word that was lost
And the word you'd throw a dog;
Transform me who travel towards infinity
In a makeshift monologue.

A Look in the Mirror

Those iron men!
The Indian wings his way upon an arrow;
Pale blue the sailor
Saunters on the sea;

And the farmer's boy,
Drinking his diesel, eats up the earth,
Spitting out the stones:
These never dwindle down in ink;

Nor Million Dollar
Heavyweights, nor does the Spaceman thrown
Against the dartboard of the moon,
For theirs are necessary capers;

These are the lovely eternal brutes:
All time's bravura, the hailed and the well;
Let us drink to them a foam of ale;
And in the glass consider you

Whom some half-truth stuns
Now autumn ravishes; yet still possessed
By the savage script of the young man,
By the savage dictation,

A heart out of plumb,
And time out of mind, his head
Turned back on his shoulders, nodding
To a drunken line.

A question then,
Why thumb a disconsolate nose
At these marvellous fellows, you with that in-looking face
Your own mirror hardly knows?

Wexford to Commodore Barry

When the story
Reaches the stage of bronze, the omens
That sang are dead too; the glory
All that remains.
It is little enough
Even when man still wears his earthly stuff.

Good Hero and
All American man, that other lord
Of spear and trumpet, Achilles, banned
And blue in Hades, put it in a word;
Death is the worst thing;
Life makes every petty drudge a king.

Do not, for God's sake,
Envy old schoonermen, your mates
On the water who can still kick:
Life too satiates,
And they have only breath
Enough to admire you for your lack of death.

In the Bally of your birth
They say no braveries were allowed;
Small houses laboured up from bits of earth,
And lest soul turn to mud,
Man thatched the things; and so, to put it raw,
Friend, Bronzefellow, you were a man of straw

With your back bent
Early. To lords and hunger you
Bowed uneasily, paying the usual rent,
Not yet thinking how
Far out beyond bondage a boy could go
Over oceans of himself to make his harbour stow.

The boy made man;
The boy who'd but a beggar's rights to the road
Threw all his thread on the open ocean
And found how threatening latitudes
Expand. Now, tall as ships can be,
On the earth's round ripple you stand up at sea.

So, Bronzefellow, we
On this waterledge find you comfort us;
Success of a kind is poetry,
A headline we miss.
'Aye', sigh some, 'our John brought home the gravy.'
But you made from the Irish chip an oaken Navy.

Deluge

The winter was without end;
The walk of youth legaway from a bogged-down calendar;
The old left behind
With the blind and the helplessly married
To climb their cocklofts and wait
For the ditchwater fields to push up another level
And the mossgreen belfry toll of itself.

That was a season
In the city and worse; the broken glass of the weather
At every corner;
People passing by with last year's faces;
The very spouts were walking,
Lovers erased, washed from the warehouse doors;
But such copulation the whores wore boots and furs.

The sea so piled, so much
It could not, swore the tidewaiters, possibly be more;
Yet such it was.
That was the time of boredom, of terrible ennuis
Afflicting virgins and true believers;
We had suffered before such inundations
Only when He numbered himself with our enemies.

And then one day
In a lane no wider than your hand a woman
Leaned out of a fug
Of food and napkins and found an air so mild
She hung the goldfinch out,
Loitering while the little bird perked up and sang
To gossip with another window over the way.

March Twentysix

All men rage in royal Lear
Poor old man,
His winter body out of plan,
His flesh antediluvian;

Knowing the perishable year
Is every old man,
And human nature out of date,
Yet clinging to the butcher's meat.

The head that guttered in the air
Is every old man
Nailed to the body, that bare tree.
Lost in the mutter of geography.

The mad white head, distracted stare
Is every old man
And fellow traveller, burnt out
And come into his second sight.

Leaves afterglows, the borrowed wear
Of every other man,
The raiment of an old mad king,
Some tattered daft Platonic thing.
All men rage in old mad Lear.

2.

We put James Starkey down today,
A few of us old friends and went our way;
The last, said we;
Gone the galaxy.

March Twentysix, a raindown day;
A blackbird yielding to one single spray;
Delicate the flute
Lifted above the mute.

Poi s'ascose nel foco
Che gli affina – there too without echo,
Sweetly undone,
Is Lesbia's sparrow, the little one.

No sweet mouth but comes to this,
God Attis too for all that Great Goddess
And heavenly stuff:
Much is man and not enough.

River Lane

1.

That girls in the river, nymphs
Aloof in the female whorl and seashell shiver,
Could ever become old women beating clothes!
That those gay whipsters, virgin born
Tuning the milkwhite unicorn
Under the singing linnet at lane doors
Should turn to old mad gossips thumb to nose.

That our Madge who had such bubble and bud
Into her latest motherhood
Forgetting that the body's lent,
Should prolong the happy time of rut,
A great bulldozing Bacchic slut
All anguish when her time was spent,
Still clinging to her instrument;

All the passions come to stay;
In love or out of it no holiday.
With little left, the wick is all.
Ridiculous Helen will blue the moon
With the shadow of her going down;
Leda in her dotage scull
A mess of feathers on a pool;

And our old drunken Madge sail out
To bully the babble in the common street;
In the square no less, filled with the itch
And opulence of the vanished myth,
And suffering some kind of death,
Shake her clothes off every stitch
To show the roses of the bitch.

What lover ever who threw on this peg
A coat of arms could sing the wagging dug,
Or see the seaborne for the crows,
Or know for truth that on this breast
Man runs, a vast historic beast,
His race between her mouth and knees
And shoots his arrows at her skies?

Precisely under the church clock
She spins for all eyes round the Zodiac.
The world stands still
While she unlocks the raven hair
In the lost youth that envelops her.
Percussion of pigeons on the chapel bell:
The town one worldwide windowsill.

A little quiet country place
Shattered by an old mad mask of savage face;
Venus Anadyomene
Gone screwy, with every churchman's shaft
Feathering her broomstick tuft;
Careless of councils and decrees
The pigeons flutter round her knees.

She has the square to herself,
Old Madge, fallen off the wagon, and off the shelf
Where the cruse of oil is rich
With the Virgin's face, and history is not
The crescent that grows and ranges round the lot
To finish its moon round such,
Occulting on a cratered crutch.

Yet a most sonorous whore;
An excess of flesh; the epic had its hour.
And now like bats she calls her twittering dead

To beak and nuzzle, the horsed Huzzar
Or maybe her first conqueror,
That Esquire in his hunting red
Who drank from her uplifted head.

2.

Piously
They say; a Rosary
In the flagrant hands; the treed God
On the gargantuan deserted mamillae:

From her house of finches,
Shouldered by six goes
Her piece of pine;
We take it in turns, each man to his trick;

She's rights in the old graveyard, so
It's round the town for us, an ancient custom;
My right shoulder aches at the stone cross;
The old drumbeat was a weight;

And I doubt if she's yet translated
From that batwinged virago, akimbo
In her bawling shawl;
The gates are open and we trample in

Where the de Burghs lie under broken
Slabs. Glass wreaths
Crunch on unkempt graves. It's noon
When we reach her upturned pile and pay her down.

Not a sob, not a face breaks, she'd gone
Far past her span, gone on, gone on
With the untimely rhetoric
Of a mastodon.

The first spadeful; a shake
Of holy water from a naggin bottle,
A Pater and Ave. (Though she died in a Mary habit
Nobody thinks she'll make it.)

Noon, and in the spare woodwork
Of December, low
As a lilac blooms suddenly the sun;
And I think maybe she did and all:

For what man ever
Quite totted up the human figure?
Here's famous holy ground at least,
And she lies at long last with the great.

The River Walk

Disturbing it is
To take your stick sedately walking
Evening in the water and the air,
And discover this; that a woman is a river.
The mythic properties are hard to bear.

Dismaying are
The ways she will intrude – if she intrude
Or merely assume the garments that you give her:
But a water willow stared at for so long
Glows graciously and knows the why you brood.

And such gesticulation –
Are you so young? – before the gentle birch
In its first shimmer: Lover, are you true
To one, or merely finding all you search
Brings the one woman home to you?

But how absurd to see
Her in that stilted bird, the heron in
A silt of river, all her blues pinned up:
In that brocaded goose the swan
For all her myths with Jupiter on top.

Dangerous, dangerous
This mythology. The doctors know it
And reason of it now like any poet.
Lover, go back no farther than your birth:
A woman is a woman, not the earth.

Her human business is
To resolve a man of other women always,
Not be, in a beautiful grotesque, all bodies
So various, a lover – if the girl insist
On love – must be a very pantheist.

A Public Appointment

He was stranding on the ripple
When she looked, the virgin. Her mute maids stood
Broadbeamed in the morning, washed, and nude as ingots,
While she went on.
The thing before her was no monstrous shell,
But a red man run over by the ocean.

She was to learn that pity was a pity
Between a man and a woman, but could she then, a virgin,
Know it, whose body heavenly Athene
Used so subtly
To break down this bull-man to her own
Particular lust – that's beyond flesh and bone?

So what the hero saw
In his run-down vision while his footsteps ranged
Around him uncontrollably as dolphins,
Was the white tower she was
And the sacred woman
In the city inside the city, unsacked Ilium.

Lustres he'd lost at sea
Would come back, he'd borne such brunts before
On his wide sea-front and taken them for granted;
But this was a new peril,
And in his weakness sweeter than the Siren,
This pity she offered him, so sisterly, so virgin.

The first look had made them
All ever they could be to one another,
Suppliant to Goddess, son to mother;
Neither was aware
Of all that was lost
Though it wept and swooned around them in the ghost.

And the girl had felt
The male in the storm that breached him, the rough pelt
Of the lover, and all the rolling bed.
But the man was down
Below the mercury; undone.
The great boomerang remained unthrown.

So Pallas Athene had her way.
Ulysses, recovered from the ocean and the blue
Barbarous tattoos of the receding god,
Was returned posthaste
To his public appointment. All
In heaven and earth bow down to protocol.

Yet when his people, shepherds
With heads in the clouds and sailors pouring water,
Demanded a statue to that sacred eloquence,
What rose up in the square
Was not oracular, no great mouthing of stones,
But the wanderer, that slender buffeted bronze.

Yes, though he died old and slowly
Into his vineyards, requiring like the sun
One whole horizon to decline upon,
The image that remains
Is the haunted man on the main of love, forever
Sailing, and beside him a virgin at the tiller.

Late Poems
(1960-1974)

An Island

A man must go naked to an island,
Let the weather lend
A skin till he grows one, the rock fit
The beat of the surftop to
His feet; let him go like spindrift
Till he find wings, or the wave
Streamline him like the great
Matter of a seal.

Let him find toes too,
Prehensile or web, for the cliff fall;
Let him put two notes in his pipe
And be the first music.
Let the island be the eye
And the boundary of his being, then
Let him be an island
And bound on his own beat,

Back before Gods,
Before the beginning, before the betrayal,
Before the woman slopped over on his bed,
Before the sun stood on a stone circle;
Let him go back to be
Just one simple thing, matter, an island
At its first meeting with the sea.

Weir Bridge

The lodestoned salmon, hurtling
Always in the right direction, find
The trickle of their birth,
Stand fantailed on the falls
And somersault into the milting weather.

Whole gravels are in rut.
The ocean has come home to melt away
The salt, to lie under
A maybush and almost tenderly
Suck from the lazy heavens a blue-green fly.

On love's seething house,
Rocking the thousand cradles, the first fresh
Will fall and the spent bulls
Drop with it down the slow river spirals;
Aching for space now the once rampant males;

Caught here in their bored
Congregations, while the wandering nerve
Twitches towards Norway. How many years
Since I first saw the stones waver,
The river paving turn to fins and tails?

Loafing a lunch hour in the sun,
And here's the wheel come round again;
So much to do, so little done;
The tiny trickle of my birth
Dwindling back into the earth.

On the Jetty

Old men bleed
Quietly into one another, the gossips
Of summer and seaweed
Unhinged now from giant epics

And with as little space as
Dead starfish, they who
Sank with the mercury down
The Pole and broke hóles in the blue

And rode their timbers out through a welter
Of geography, die slowly.
What they made was rich
But has no history

And leaves nothing, no body
That might reverberate
Like the small whorled compass of a shell
That stacked away a world of light;

Hobbling aboard the stone jetty,
Crutched and woolled, they cackle to their peers;
Conches they need, sea-trumpets
To bring back the bellowing years,

Not this uncertain pianissimo
To winter arteries and the dead leaves
Of their shredded hands;
Their number less by tomorrow. And who grieves

Outside the ever dwindling circle?
Who'll understand
Their mountains of water, or their daily
Victories far off land?

Gowran Park, Autumn Meeting

The year's potatoes, they've ploughed them out,
The threshing rig's gone round about;
Earth finishes with the harvest time.

A low sun noses through the damps;
The trees are bare down to the stumps;
A mist can spring up white as lime.

The fox is red as the huntsman's coat,
The doublebarrel rhymes a note,
The season turns on the hill;

But day sits up like a hunkered hare
As horse and jockey catch the roar;
Gowran lights like a paper spill.

Soon long shadows will creep from the grill
Of every gate, the mountains stamp,
The year fall into the Christmas lamp.

Fin de Siècle

He'd seen them off, some down
The gutters of the stews,
Scarcely awake, sad drunks
And disastrous lovers as they say;
He'd seen the manias take over;
And even Wilde, for all
His heraldry, die maudlin:

Never his hailfellows exactly;
Golden boys to whom
The Muses hearkened at the well already,
And the rampant horse came
At the first call;
They were the early promisers
High upon the swaying feathers

At a time when he
Was kicking along the old gelded spavin,
Mild as a monk, they were high up there
Engaging the whole heaven;
Icarus had a like fall, melting
Down before anything big could happen;
But those were the Muse driven

Who'd seen the shocking vision and lived on
Those were the harassed
And the lost;
In the wide world no comforter:
Into the earth's dumb side
The big horse stamped them, waiting
For the next victim, the next master,

Who was you-know-who,
The unlikeliest, like the lucky youngest brother
Whose faery godmother said: 'Go slow!
Take it easy;
Disaster
Is the portion of the young. Who lives long
Enough will make a master.'

Out on the periphery he put in the time;
Achilles dead, and Hector, Ulysses flown
And he the brighter for the falling bolts.
Who makes the rhyme
Will have the resonance. Carefully
He lived to tell the tale;
Homer is he who survives the crumbling wall.

He shakes a carefully shaggy head;
Oddly he is not comforted;
The years round on him;
The unspent shekels jangle in
The too-careful flesh. Oh the abandon
They had, who were all mad youth,
Suicide and singing mouth.

They troop by, uncalled. The wanton
Stares are bright; Shades are reasserting
The sole right of Youth, which is
Merely to be beautiful.
The mockery.
This old body wandering on his wall,
Mock tower, mock battlements,
And out there all the glory of the fall;

And the abyss, the horse
No longer mild and nickering. Try the ride,
Old body, be
The most famous suicide.
A bit unsound in wind, heavy of limb,
He rises from his years, to find
A great carnivorous creature under him.

The Young Fenians

They looked so good;
They were the coloured lithographs
Of Murat, Bernadotte and Ney
And the little Corsican.
Mars had made them from our dead
And given to each his martial head.

The cavalry and plumes would come,
No doubt about it;
Every half-acre man with a sword,
The boy with a drum;
And down the Alps of every local hill
The bannered horses ride to kill.

O'Connell helpless in the house;
The old gazebos at their talk,
All to no purpose;
Tone must rise and Emmet walk,
Edward troop out of Kildare;
The time had come; the day was fair.

Flags flew from our every word;
The new names sang from litanies,
Saviours each one;
They were the eagles in the morning sun;
A country rising from its knees
To upset all the histories.

Capricornian

In a quiet place,
Sea-locked, the moon is the pendulum
And the year the only face
Scanned for time;
The figures turn through the sun
Twelve ancients stand on the horizon.

Nearer than the twelve
Gazebos in their old star houses
Is the ram that rounds his horn on the hill;
The stone donkey by the wall
Is humble, has no wings; Taurus
Never stamped a cow like my black bull;

And my mother goat steps daintily
From ledge to ledge, ignores the fabulous
Ocean; she

Too is no heraldry, offers us
A full udder to fill the cans and
Occasionally brings forth twins

The old people love
To dine on, like
That old poet with his Falernian. He, too,
Found spring wells holy, some
God hung above
The natural bubble, his bright kingdom come;

Feared the sea god
Who locks havens, the sky piled
With wilder fellows, the uncontrollable;
Yet on a May day from the gorse
The eyes see fairly
A peopled sea, the hulls in a haze of morse;

And from our wedge
Of world, here on the very edge
Feel the one and the various move upon the spindle,
But the god singular,
An islandman
Who touches the chimney pots with smoke, who is a
    calendar

Of everyday affairs, a neighbour's voice,
A woman at the churn,
A child in wonder at the half door,
The split pollock drying in the sun,
The boats pulled up and
All night the moon, the pendulum.

A Visit West

The town is an ideogram
Of a town with its square keep and the brush of smoke
From the baker's chimney,
Almost intact at first sight
With wall and moat and narrow gate.
The wooden horse is in the square.

Everywhere my uncle Ben
Emerges with a limp from a round tower;
And that's the poem I'd like to write,
The old boy tipping his rod to the wavy weather,
Fish hooks and feathers thrown
Over the windy edge of March;
He owns them all now, the streaming rivers
By inalienable right.

So humbly down the river lawn
I'd tail him with a tuppenny pole;
(Hare's Ear, March Brown)
Here was a soul who lived alone;
Gone before I'd reach the bridge
Far off on a desolate slab of sky
Tipped off the harsh Atlantic roof,
Fly size.

The wooden horse is in the square.
Urbs, they say, intacta, meaning
The virgin sleeps late;
Between yawns life goes on
With some cunning to
Accomplish itself.

Children are born,
To up and vanish like me,
Mostly;
There is no return, and the wound
There and leaching
Forever into the one and
Only summer;

Lost.
The wooden horse is in the square;
And Ben, old Ben.

2.

To pay off the ghost, two
Bottles of brandy
Left with the nuns to dole out
Circumspectly;
White coif and wimple, heavenly
Barmaids.

What greater wrong could I have done
On this cantankerous spirit
Limping in from nowhere with nuts and trout
And wild apples
Who'd get most nobly drunk on a market day!

What now he's gone?
New slates and paintwashed shops,
A garage in a flower bed;
Hovel and seeding thatch swept from the lane
And the hag's head
Curing slowly on
The smoking half door, like ham.

3.

He saw a lingering eighteenth century out,
The great mansions left
Embedded in the prosy land
Die of their heraldry;
Even saw the last rebellion start,
The wooden horse stand in the square.

And never gave the world a thought
As the vast familiar glacier melted down;
While Kaisers fell and navies sank he drowned
His pint glass in Glynn's
Tallied his ewes abroad, his dog
Tucked at his heel, the West

Tumbling over him, his own sky
Strung from his fist.

Original
Inhabitant or feckless double
Opting out with his toy town and
Baby river,
An old primitive do-nothing who
Stabilised among the lesser shades
Can still pull

Me over the Shannon to lose me in
His greenery where the grass
Watches of the fields are stalled
Forever

And time is March and bright
Elysium
Where he disappears, his body gone
Into the weather
Without a care.

The wooden horse stands in the square.

Boyne Valley

On a mound chipped
From the dead, deity
And scantlings dismantled, the spell broken,
I stand on a stone ship
That sails nowhere

But once was set right to launch
The bronze and brandished hero, fellow
Of this same sun that low now
In bare twigs
Lies lumped in the winter's wicker basket,

Who was laid in
This hill of metaphor, as if a grave has no end,
Suspended in some state of grace above
His own diving depths
To find North like the barnacle

And a quite definite eternal Paradise
(Only the best admitted, Stags
Of the year, Gods
In the demi-brackets) not very different from this;
But Paradise is always somewhere else,

Leaving his head to the stone axe, and the big, broken
Torque of his body to dangle,
Wail, ye women,
God is dead
And picked over by this year's summer students,

Whose secret name was
A flight of months, the whole earth offering
Its barbarous alphabet to make him delicate;
Now trees and stones have forgotten; the birds
Are entirely without auspices

And preen flit strut in winter attitudes,
Birds, not litanies. The thing is gone
Now that no giant drops from the gaudy zenith
Like Mad Sweeney
To hang on the last Elder tree head and antlers.

Flayed, to be scattered in this the thirteenth
Unlucky month, for Fertility, for a patch
Of emmer barley, for all men –
To give their guts literally to this, –
To Demeter the first plough.

A sow, snouted with the moon's horn! But
It's Isis I think of, Magna Mater, to whom
The divine members from their schism clambered;
Into the magnet they came, the brilliant head
Topping the whole winged tread again –

Meaning just a new sun
On the old wheel, the one wheel, and world safe inside
The big roll of gravity, but
Aware there is a moment
When all things could fall in,

As indeed they may,
For all this peaceful scene, Boyne cease to flow
Broad through this green valley with
Its copious flood
Of ephemeral nature notes,

Such as one swaying sunheaded reed,
Such as a crow daubed on the ripple of
A black poplar, a thrusting ash
In its hedgeleap carrying
The long horizon on a twig, twice.

Distantly a horn, not Herne and his hounds but
Esquires at play, a near hill rolls gold
For some unearthly reason,
And maybe too this battered helmet of a place
I straddle cold

With sheep suddenly on the fosse;
Souls? No, merely ewes
And wearing the ram's pigments, the autumn's raddle;
Fertility minds its own business;
And world will go on more or less

The same notwithstanding God
Or Goddess; only man the danger. Still
It must be heartening in ill times to have
Ties with the whole network,
God on the wire inside a hill.

Jaguars roll from the meet, trailing
Horseheads and dogfoxes. History
Is slowly reaching some conclusion somewhere;
And here is the usual tentative dusk
As day runs out of silver

And one flintnebbed swan owns all the Boyne;
No afterglow or
Gold bowl to sail home the antlered one,
Surrogate, heraldic sufferer,
Cernunnos, Arthur, Bran.

Kiltartan Legend

Penelope pulls home
Rogue-lord, artist, world wanderer,
Simply by sitting in a house,
Its sturdy genius;
Of all sirens the most dangerous.

She'll sit them out,
The curious wonders, the ventriloquial voices,
Spacious landfalls, the women, beds in the blue;
Her oceanography
The garden pond, her compass a knitting needle.

The arc-lamped earth, she knows,
Will burn away and she
Still potter among her flowers waiting for him;
Apollo runs before
Touching the blossoms, her unborn sons.

Knitting, unknitting at the half heard
Music of her tapestry, afraid
Of the sunburned body, the organs, the red beard
Of the unshipped mighty male
Home from the fairy tale;

Providing for him
All that's left of her she ties and knots
Threads everywhere; the luminous house
Must hold and will
Her trying warlord home.

Will she know him?
Dignity begs the question that must follow.
She bends to the web where her lord's face
Glitters but has no fellow
And humbly, or most royally, adds her own.

Yeats at Athenry Perhaps

1.

We had our towers too, a large
Stone soldiery at bridge and gateway, they
Were the whole town once;
And I could have nodded to him from the top
Tendril of ivy or a jackdaw's nest;
But I'd never heard of him, the famous poet,
Who lived as the crow flies fifteen miles away.

Certainly he'd have touched us changing trains
For Gort, have hours to idle, shared
The silence of our small town shell;
Maybe he passed me by
In a narrow-gutted street, an aimless
Straying gentleman, and I
The jerseyed fellow driving out the cows.

Ours was a sightseeing place that had
Exhausted history, but old wars had left
A dead king and a moat
And walls still half alive that watched
From towers with broken rims. I doubt
He bothered with us, all his sight turned in;
Some poems come better waiting for a train.

And that winged footprint could have jarred
The peasant metres of a street given over
To baker, grocer, butcher and
The treadmill of the till. What would he think
Of our outcropping sheds, the architecture
Of the very necessary animal?
And little better our weathered Famine chapel?

But on the eve of May he might have found
Things near his heart, Fertilities
Dropping in;
For then from consecrated ground we moved
The Virgin to the leafing trees
With bonfires, chanting children, the whole works;
The Canon hadn't read the latest books
On golden boughs and odd divinities.

Or would he have looked superior, been difficult
About Our Lady's face, the soft Italian
Look of the milking mother, not the sort
That strings the whole air like a catapult?
This was no moon in women, no
Unpredictable lady sailing
Her wavy shell;
Ours kept the house and answered the chapel bell.

Or so we thought or didn't think at all.
Diana has her secrets from the oak;
The nunlike night commits itself in strokes
Of barbarous shorthand when the candles die.
What's fifteen miles? We could have read together
The same nightscript, felt the vibrations run,
Boughs singing, with the whole south moving up
To stand in a dripping arch of spring.

2.

I'd like to think how over the sheep and crops,
The nut-creggs and the loose stone walls we met
In a mutual hazard of burning arrows, but
I was too small then, my wavelengths caught
In anything low-down as a hawthorn tree
And jammed there for a day or all the summer,
Time no object, profession poetry.

Anyway he wouldn't have dared a town
Where every peeling window was an eye;
We smiled of course at strangers, proud
Of a dead king, the lordly
Dung that simmered in the ground. But I could
Have walked him round the moat, in Kingsland shown the rock

113

Where the crown toppled from the last Irish head
And a royal footsole left a bloody track.

No, he'd have sat down by the line and waited
Melting his bits of ore or watched the sky
Jolt from the saltmills of the Atlantic over
A town that died so often of the rain;
Why muddy a feathered foot when a great house waited
Over in Coole among the trees
(He liked his heraldry alive, well baited)
With all the amenities for Muse and man,
Leda's kingbird on a lake, a lawn
For Juno's peacock, tranquil as a frieze.

Stop on the Road to Ballylee

I read Horace here
Where the lunatics now shamble around
The wrong side of their shadows. Kore or the moon
Have no pity. Mouthfuls of air,
Said the Big Tower, that's what we are.

Q. Horatii Flacci Carminum Liber 1;
Elementary classics, small blue book, Macmillan.
Our soft Cs were true Italian.
                        These
Overlay the place, shamblers
Stuck with the upper air,

Illustrating something, limbo or something, not
Like Liber 1 with its fauns and coins, Spring
(After a Pompeian wall painting;
At the woman's unsubtle nipple the first lamb yawns)
As if they saw behind the scenes

Not the Discus Thrower, page 9 –
From a marble in the Palazzo Lancelotti –
Never that, no more, or the Greek boy with the jaculus, my own
Age, page 10;
              I tossed it too but antiquity magnifies.
Inward or outward these eyes?

Eight of us that drank the air here.
Now joy is difficult (like Beauty), but the big tower would have us
Make our verse like his, sing
Jubilant Muses. And these sad quidnuncs
Sidling by and round some broken thing,

Avoiding commitment; some woman laid them
Low or they denied her, Mater Saeva
Cupidinum – what ode?
                              Some fellows sacked for her, plucked
                              burning
After lights out from the sidereal bush
(In the haggard with a skivvy, in the hay)

Flagrante dilecto behind the fawnstoned ballalley
And sacked. What end to those fellows?
The bogmaidens walked away with some fine scalps.
(For the matter in an ode, to penetrate to
The great beat, thrown out, lost extra muros)

And these are husked, the flail is on them, unbuttoned
The only seamless garment, it is the dinginess
Hurts, affronts.
And Hermes (curvae lyrare parens) fashioning the toy
For love and the echoes of, for resonance;

Lynx lion tree-stumped, flamingo
Grounded by that lute, and the hells too in suspension,
Held up by a lover, Orpheus page 13
Where the dead hung off like these from the barbarous new ghost
With all that sounding metaphor, like these, the lost

Who still drift in the old flesh, confusing the
Gods, who no longer sing to their own wires
Or hang together
In the beat that is one beat, the all-beat.
Eight we were in the fine young weather;

Bright flashes, and some gone down Earth's
Hollow foundations.
                              (That other Hermes, the conductor, what
Page, psychopompus, with a soul for Charon's fishprow)
Time to go now, time to be on the way.
(That was a woman the winghatted God had in tow)

Reminding me of that old girl being led away
Half dead at the top and too much down below.
Graveclothes the heavy skirts she heaped up to her navel,
The raw focus of it, and they bundled her away,
Poor soul not down yet to the ultra violet ghost,

In the main Asylum grounds O years ago
                              Edited by T.E. Page,
A prig but he did leave Faunus that field artillery.
Something came through,
A name, a coin, a winged horse,
Inked over by yours truly where they walk now,

The unburied
Illustrating something, Limbo or something, the unregarded
Who underlie us.
                    Three measures
Of clay and we're at liberty to leave
To lay our tin wreaths on more iambic matter
At the Big Tower (those centenaries)
In Ballylee, Ballylee,
Through Loughrea and Kilchreest where my own kin lie strewn
In the all mothering weathering Galways skies,
To a dead swan in Leda's thighs.

On the Tower Stairs

1.

Arrow slits with heads
Of bitter weather; even here on this
Stone spindle winding up I have to think of her,
A dugout deity, a disconcerting
Earth mother living on.

Outwardly just a plain
Dump of a woman; no planetary body this
To magnify or disintegrate, genius
To no man. Yet Symons
All crow and ominous had sensed the siren

That afternoon she'd dropped in at Tulyra
Where he and Yeats were summering. 'La Strega',
Quoth the Temple Beau sniffing
The quite ordinary meat –
Which makes no witch of her and no carnivorate.

Nor a Beardsley black and white
Alive with insomnia in
Her widowed woods and swanlake. This was a lady
Given to no love
But a house and the glory thereof;

Stumping her walks for boundary and trespass;
And there was a diary
Voluminous, with the low trajectory
Of the Galway grass; and there was this
(Mr. Gregory's Postbag) biography

Of a long-gone dismal hack who'd dined
On the Castle periphery, another of the husband-father
Who from a simple
Bible household bare
As a tent translated her

To rooms where books
Were accepted inhabitants. He'd held the gorgeous
East in fee, somewhere a governor
Before her time –
Ceylon, I think, where the tea comes from

And elephants dance round Buddha's tooth.
Take it easy, this
Is a serious lady ready for a new
Dispensation. Did she know it
Watching him the gangling poet

In square, or is it trine, with Martyn's woods
Which rumour had it he was rocking
Some nights with lunar incantations?
What did she see
Beyond the too obvious anarchy,

Locust buzz and face of honey? The prophet authentic,
Like Midsummer John all lovely head?
Divining in
The endless budding of the wand
A lord of wine?

What were her chances?
A man with an arrow in his heart and a lifetime woman
More turbulent than a Muse;
And she with her cruse of oil half spent, in
The crepuscular shiver of the menopause?

2.

A dumpy vernacular Victoria
Ruminating homewards to her moated bed,
(The very road I took this morning
In the downpour)
How did she manage it, capture the speaking head?

Maud Gonne from her hawklegged heights at eighty laughing
(Never in this tower she, never
On this stair)
'She did try to play Kathleen...but
She lisped so badly, poor dear.'

Vanity? (That bronze
In Charlemont House?) What does it matter now?
Who can question the work done?
I stand in the rainblitzed light
Outside, in the dogstare of the door.

Her trumpeted house is gone, entirely razed;
But he did raise up another
There on the totem pole in which the lady is
Oracular and quite composed
To outlast everything, live on forever.

Letter from Ballylee

Raftery, a tramp poet,
Sung for the thatches around the homespun girl
Whose name was Mary Hynes:
Later, of course, the beauty was debauched
By some hard-riding nameless
Country gentleman,
And died lost and wrinkled in
A bog cabin.

The girl goes always to the other fellow.
Exalt no girl, my friend;
Flesh no arrow. Witness this man who plumps anew
The old stone shell by the river.
Now he sings of God and lesser things
And studies planetary ebb and flow
Who saw Helen leave the high wall for
A quite ordinary lover.

He gets by, like
A hermit crab who blunders in from the blue
Bristle of the sea.
Waiting a new skin he hears
The old shell singing. Pitiful
The story, how an old love can discompose us.
Perhaps I should sing God too
And the partial planets, did this girl allow me
Who puts me at the disposal of the Muses.

The Small Town of John Coan

1.

Invent them for us,
The open storeys overhead: we need
Them, the overplus, the changing
Bodies and a new seed.

Let Olympus overhang the street
And gossips will be poets. I want to see
Cornuted bulls, and amorous
Birds in the family tree.

Strict biology
Caters to no truth we need. Who hid
In Juno's robes
Begat a god

And time and things like towns
That burned famously and battles that would yield
Hubbub and talk enough
For any man in a field:

Give us the lady's name
Who hides in the golden shower; boredom
Is where we lie now, with never a window
On Messalina's Rome;

And the sad river never
Manages to be Cydnus, never will float
Even in dream pharaoh's
Daughter or gilded boat.

Amoris domina, saddle this
Golden ass to break through to the tale
Of new dimensions;
Mother of love, command another Fall,

New Eve, new Adam, a new tree,
Gardens where nymphs are
Stories of air and water; let there be
Pipes in the air,

The cobble break
Into the blue, the town tumble into apple
Blossom, the Graces nude and linked
Lead out the season in a dancing rabble.

2.

And just when he was all in it,
From head to foot the welling heartbeat,
This thing, this town, ceased to articulate for him.
Some ogre behind the font?
Some field god tired of making wheat?

Shocked when a child sister
Was walked in her deadbox to the old church
He saw the light turn sinister:

Some one had moved the morning
With an almost invisible lurch
And set it down askew.

Afterwards certainly all world was
Out of the true
Morning after morning.

3.

Semele's son
Squandered to the riot buds in a field,
His privates blown, a no-man
Dowsed and spelled:

The unplotted torso swells; in the round
Of the year he rolls, reason enough for those
Revolving set-pieces; and in demand,
Season burgeoning from season; every woman his.

Autre temps,
          What so eager happens now?
What neighbour hill is begging me to die,
Offering endless resurrections?

Now spring is harnessed to a commonplace,
What rose glows in Cancer? What boy's face
In the empty stubble can autumn contemplate?

4

The portrait of Mrs O
Overall is black with
One eye bead sunken in
A beaked shawl.

The eye's the thing, receiver of
Dismembered cities if needs be. There
The Town is
Upside down in the harsh indifferent glare.

She broods in sombre areas; pruned
To crucifixion are the trees in her garden;
She stands on all the ways out in some

Survival like rock, won't go
Into water colours ever; simply shares
Her matter with some old-fashioned status quo.

The Christmas Vigil

Wherever else the real miracle
Was happening, with climates curtsying
To the small holy city, out here
On the west periphery
Our Galway weather hadn't nodded east.

Elsewhere the nub
And circles of rejoicing heaven, stars high and low
Lifting to the skyline
The figures of donkey, man and virgin
Moving towards Bethlehem.

So, on the old cart
Bumping on the road by Lopdells, today
Had not arrived, the trees
With aboriginal arms still making
Yesterday's rain

From the day's soft grey substance; no
New magnitude in the stone
Fields, no distances starting to flow
Into rainbows; there was only this
Same old world with yesterday's leftovers.

All the way to Mountbawn, with
Bullocks in a horned frieze staring
Egyptian from the roughmasoned gateways, ours
Storming the cart as we appeared;
We tossed them their turnips and went wheeling

Over the usual earth. Obviously
Christmas had not come to the brutes on this
Waterhaunted ledge of the Atlantic. It
Was quiet in the lambing paddocks, the ewes
Waiting at the troughs

In sops of gold straw for the broken oats;
And we dished it out, we two
Shepherds of sorts though no sky would open
For Nicholas Moran pipe in mouth now
And quite happy in his wingless span

Of Galway clay. Me too, for miracles belong
Over the ultimate horizon; nothing here
Has learned the rudiments,
No beast of ours
Drizzling over his fat roots will turn celestial,

Unlike the Bible ox
In the crib under the organ gallery, where
With a star strung like a kite above
And the new lunation in its eye,
The beast lights up with human love.

But this is the mystery welling
Up from some inner world in a sort
Of perennial heartbeat. All day the glow of it
Fills the back of my mind; but I won't look;
Not yet

Being simply afraid of what could happen.
I like things as they are,
World as it is, the wonder just round the corner;
And if at midnight
All the clocks in the world meet to chime

Over the world's newest child, this
Will be the more spacious for happening in my sleep
Where ends can meet in peace
When the great harps sweep out upon the pediments
And the wren waken with a tiny cheep.

Mater Dei

In March the seed
Fell, when the month leaned over, looking
Down into her valley.
And none but the woman knew it where she sat
In the tree of her veins and tended him
The red and ripening Adam of the year.

Her autumn was late and human.
Trees were nude, the lights were on the pole
All night when he came,
Her own man;
In the cry of a child she sat, not knowing
That this was a stranger.

Milk ran wild
Across the heavens. Imperiously He
Sipped at the delicate beakers she proffered him.
How was she to know
How huge a body she was, how she corrected
The very tilt of the earth on its new course?

The House

I stare at it again;
One should remember one's own birth, the first
Fact. The act
Of creation begins there
Where the apple burst.

It's empty air
More or less, the place built over
And a new house settled down
With a shop on the ground floor.
The man born here is a displaced person

And can act only
If up there, an inset in the first storey,
The weightless midwife still
Removes him from the womb, the outrage
Accomplished but unending, never final.

So let candles go
About the four brass knobs, the mother lie
Broad as the seventh day at peace with me;
A flowery wallpaper encloses her
Above the gulps of geography;

Far east, Port Arthur and the yellow threat
Of the little ricemen, battleships gone down;
And the day so mild here and drifting
Soft airs from Clare, the bare trees
Budding rain. History is made at home

Such as it is, and the round world
Established incessantly, like me from you,
On crumbling fronts, instant history
Up to the last pain and the final assault on
The tower of your modesty.

It was late and long
When I came you said, the leaking balloon
Of day deflated in the fields, eight
By the clock or near it, a moon
Occulted in Capricorn, the shuddering sign

That bears Christs and splits the calendar;
Eight by the clock and from my lodging in you
I issued forth
To take up residence in the usual fears,
Loves and longings of the starbacked earth.

Lean back now and still,
Labour just over, the teapot on the hob;
Ignore the signs.
That big black head may be heretical,
But you did your job.

Lean back I say, forever there,
My passport into things;
Name the world for me, who passes by
Name the mudladen streets and who drops in;
And name your son who's starting to begin.

Monument X

Stone has gone, no
God clamours nowadays to be
Let out, or even to beat
Inside barbarously in the menhir's heart.
Stonehenge is archaeology.

Unlike that old raw
Obelisk where all streets meet
In the middle of my town, origin
Unknown; Galway masons
Helped it struggle to its feet,

Or I hope so, for
It belongs. Countrymen heel carts
There and pen sheep, boys
Play marbles; sometimes
Old women sit there with baskets

Of fowl, eggs, fish; and politicians
Make speeches after Mass.
Mostly, however, it survives alone,
A weather buttress, dowsing all the rains
Of the green run-down littoral,

But coming out drowsily into
The sun, with the meanings of an old man
Or a shell leftover, something gone
That beat once,
Like a poem in

A lost language like early Erse, this being
The one battered indecipherable stanza
Surviving. And it's only now
I begin to be curious. My God,
I think, is there something that I missed,

Some saint lying in
The state of God, a mine still working
Gold under us that we have forgotten,
Who never made the pious book
Like those of Syria or Antioch,

Liguria, Carthage, or High Germany,
Like Ursula, Thecla, Donato of Arezzo,
Clement, Susanna, Felicitas,
Blaise of Sebaste, barely glimmering,
And the seven Sleepers of Ephesus,

Innumerable lights
Of what never was on land or sea,
A fugue of heavenly figures
In sarcophagi like this, martyrs blessed
With names that have come down to us.

And I remember
Trooping to the top of the stone just
Such a galaxy. Or do I? My God,
I've sat there in patched shorts,
In the very weather of the thing, and must

Scratch my head to remember if
They were there
Clambering stiffly out of the masonry up
To some miracle above
In the grey Galway air:

And I can't remember now
If our rough masons summitted the job
With a cross that caught the whole East, or
With a blunt piece of Galway stone
Fathered forth some local Priapus.

Which is discouragingly ambiguous
And proves nothing except I'm not the man
I thought I was.
Still, some saints were oddly built,
Like Januarius,

Protector of Naples, Bishop
Of Benevento, who, thrust into fire
By the bloody Pagan walked out whole,
And nobody saw how in the martyr
Two faces clashed beneath the mitre.

Others had older shadows too,
The mast-top twins igniting in the blast
Above the shipping? Enough of that.
Gods live the deaths of one another.
But stone, now, is old hat.

Poet Passing

Never heed this idle fellow. Tool
Your forks, knives and wet spoons around
The pink geranium; shine
Steadily in those meagre constellations and
Dish up for your man:
Keep those bare arms out of the window pane.
The heavens are jealous of the woman
Who suddenly becomes a poem.

Like this it starts, two arms
Tending the beam, the rest of you
Unseen as yet, unborn. Bathsheba showed no more,
And there was adultery.
Watch out now, his nose is in the weather,
Antennae twinkle on the buzzing head,
Now the myths will bounce you off
The moon or some odd marriage bed.

There, he stops his gallop. Doom sealed
You're for it, lady. Tomorrow you'll
Articulate another body, be
Canzone or country ballad. Your own man won't know
Your decent rump.
Goddess, kitchenwoman, whore
Fare no better with this pimp
Who translates all into his mighty hunger;

And even now burgles
Your modest garden, where
Your intimate washing dances on the line
No lecherous bible king has eyes like his;

But how they girate for him, the
Simple cloths, the many
Indefinite nymphs you are
Holding forth upon a bit of twine!

And how he hangs over
The wall, the sea-shelled lime, the native stone.
Under the low apple how the air
Wantons with you, lady. How
Lost he is in wonder.
No man has ever seen you thus, no other
But the openmouthed zephyrs ever
Received you so loud and clear.

Great God, he's at the door now.
A cup of milk? A drink of water? Fly, or
Contain yourself, my dear, in
Your own simple fiction.
The woman suffers metamorphosis
Who heeds this tough.
That's how the story goes.
He finds like the vine a thousand soft dark eyes

That plead for him. He's all
Libation now and ceremony, shy,
Desperate as the young stag horned in the tree.
But mark that eye,
He's on the run, lady. Never
Will he belong to any other
But the virgin breast and great white limb
The goddess who set the dogs at him.

Coat of Arms

On Sundays the marvel
Was there early, like
A white stag in the grazing. Up the long
Lane to the belfry we children hung
On the feet of an old Mass-going man;
And it was making;
It was our turn to be looked upon

As if for once we
Had some distinction, the fields unyoked and
Turned loose, all occupation gone
But the business of man
In the holy city
That had no spires
Visible or choirs, a faint angelic land.

Nevertheless we
Stand there in a tree of neighbours,
Our feet in the
Broken artery of a bog village
Till the bell summoned us
To the other side of
The walled world that could be ours.

And I am already afraid
And suffering a mystery
That turns cold the faces the summer sun
Edges gold;
The strong are down upon their knees,
The ogham heads are
Bowed to the happenings on an altar stone.

Heraldic the
Manwoman who
Feeds the fire there, dilating into
Hands that lift, bless, flow:
We belong to a journey into air;
Bell and gong
Announce our presences elsewhere.

Come back.
I sweat it at the side
Of Sunday man, feeling the static shake
In a tide of invocations. Now Monday seems
Most kindly for its implements
And farm animals, all men
At home in the homely house of flesh

Drudging in stone fields
Or high on the creeled cart marketing.
Miracle is
The priest's portion
And the Latin
That came down the muletrack where Hannibal
Stalled with his elephants.

It ends;
Missa est, and
What was to be accomplished is done;
Deflates with the harmonium;
But not quite, for out there
Hanging in the blue or
Alighted in the unyoked fields is a Sunday air

Mild and
Antlered in trees, that follows
And retreats, that will neighbour us
All day, our playfellow
And almost come to hand;
And begone by tomorrow when
Monday takes over the land.

Magna Mater

A dove plus an
Assenting virgin is
An odd equation; the bird of Venus, the
Shotsilk woodhaunter and
A country shawl
In congress to produce
The least erotic of the gods.

Afoot on Sunday, walking green
The little roads or high
In the spring carts, they come to Mass;
Hundreds who know man,
For whom no string was plucked
Or any heavens
Thrown open;

No dichotomy
Affects the prayer; that heaven
Should have one love, and earth another seems
Entirely natural.
What Troubadour
Built this country chapel?

And out of what
Substance? Harping on what nerves?
Mothers here
All virgin, fathers none,
The child a gift of heaven
And held in common by
Each virgin mother.

O indestructible
Country mulch the Muses tread
So delicately, into the earth you go
Breeding, tending
Where flowers are born with the names of kings
You never heard of, pagan fellows
Whose histories and business
Are open secrets in your
Sunshining faces.

For Paddy Mac

1.

Once, so long ago,
You used to probe me gently for the lost
Country, sensing somehow in my airs
The vivid longlipped peasantry of
Last century

And those bronze men pushed
With their diminishing herds far out on
The last ledge of original earth,
Fomorian types
In the big one-eyed sky

All messed up with sundogs and
Too many rainbows, and that wishwashing head of Bran
In the toppling arches seaward sailing and singing
On his weathered maypole from
A caved-in skull.

Ours were the metres
Of early waters, the first argosy hardly home
With new women, orgies
When the moon rode round
Stone circles counting her twelve.

Homer's people,
And wasn't I lucky, born with
Boundaries floating, language still making
Out of the broadlands where my fathers
Tended their clouds of ewes?

Bunkum, Dear P. The thing was gone, or
Never was. And we were the leftovers,
Lord-ridden and pulpit-thumped for all our wild
Cudgels of Gaelic. Ours was Lever's
One-horse country; the bailiff at the bighouse door.

And hags hung all day
In turfsmoke among the fowl where I was licked.
That was a town
Walled and towered as Troy, and never sieged for a woman:
Trading bullocks and pennies for glory gone;

And watched from the top of a shilling the homespun fellows
Selling their spades on hiring days,
For a year and a day the dear flesh off their bones
From penury to slavery,
The soul thrown in for a spare.

That was my country, beast, sky, and anger:
For music a mad piper in the mud;
No poets I knew of; or they mouthed each other's words;
Such low powered gods
They died, as they were born, in byres.

Oh, maybe some rags and tatters did sing.
But poetry, for all your talk, is never that simple,
Coming out of a stone ditch in the broadlands
Newborn, or from
The fitful pibroch of a lonely thorn,

Or old saws at winter fires.
Muted the big words. Love was left
To eloping earls or such
Lest the snake creep up, usurping the ancient timber
And some odd bloom come bursting from the Cross.

2.

And you speak of Raftery, that bold tongue, the tramp
In borrowed bootleather, those rainy eyes
Lifted to empty heaven from a blind man's stick;
I sang like him you say, and praised women,
And I had the true cow's lick;

You who should know how every poet must
Baptize first the font and the very waters,
And have no godfathers but this great thirst
For what is not;
And no mothers;

Who must quote Ambrose crookedly (Nam quid divinus
Isto ut puncto exiguo culpa cadet
Populi), bog Latin for
The bit of earth we tread
Into metaphor.

Knowing we're just another civilisation
To be dumped, but go on, say it you,
We've eaten all the gods yet bow the knee,
And are only really at home
In the larger toleration of the poem.

Carefully, now that you are dead,
I must amend the scribbles of the tribe
Lest sheepman and bullhead
Become a frieze of fathers like stone man,
Hieratic, almost Egyptian,

And from the uncreated, with arms widespread,
From puncto exiguo, beyond the dead
And Lazarus rising, where God is making still
Release the flood
Of living images for good and ill.

Dear P. I'll never know
What you brought over and passed on,
But this seems certain as I grow:
Man lives; Gods die:
It is only the genuflection that survives.

Lost Man

In an old green book, mouldering
From the window ledge, sitting under
A lamp globe made in Bohemia,
I read once how to grow turnips;

In a tiny thatched house where a ladder
Cocked up to a loft above the kitchen,
Simple as the first working skeleton,
Warm as the breastwork of a pigeon;

With a cobbled yard to the little local road
That was kitchen too with a sky roof,
Ruled by an old matriarch who still spun wool
On a wheel of bog oak:

Byres, carthouses, turfricks, pigsties,
The place was open as a bird's nest
To the weather, the fields, the planetary animals,
The sun had his corner like another beast.

Neighbours too, nodding in, or high
On a creeled cart, mobile in a geography
That never moved till Sunday
Were names, roots, lineage, graphs and grafts of the one tree,

Our gossips, our daily dialogue; in
An odd way too the faces of their fields
Showed through them, the tilt of thatch or turfrick
An aura about them, their identities.

So reading by the bright wick, with
A large moth tapping out the vague
Morse of a summer's night
And the old lady at her steady wheel

Earth rolled small enough to
Be caught in the heartbeat. It was small
As I and manageable, spun to no savage foot;
And my need was to be rooted in the soil

I knew, with a village for a capital,
A spire on Sunday where a local God
Woke up to find some majesty above
The weather or the weekday sod

Where in his working clothes, in grace and grain
And grass he forgot his cherubim and trumpets,
Walked boundaries, was amenable to ewes
And quiet moonbodies like fat turnips.

Mine, of course, was a crop that never grew,
Or could be grown,
Being a life where an old girl used a wheel
Of bog oak, adze-hewn

And sand-honed by a country master long
Before the making of her world
Who laboured by diplight or hearth's glow
Till the thing worked.

Special for Nancy's Mother

Gentle lads, I know
Big moments are
Bodies with heartbeats, outlasting
Sun, moon and star;

That hill-struck with
The sheepmen, high
The weather perches on your looks,
The mountain stares you squarely in the eye;

And is yours, all
The youth and the big views of
Small boys become soul
And love

Where, up here and forever,
Boys you are,
Bodies of place and moments
You scarcely remember

Which are your life now and
Illumination;
Death being merely
Life's big double, the larger twin,

And you still happen,
Wake with morning on
The top pastures, push
The boat into the sun,

Are two brothers with a sister, are
Scree and sky
Between the two waters,
Are all the eye

Ever beheld or the heart felt;
Day never done,
Night still a golden place
With a sleeping sun.

So, dear boys, having all
The footprints, welcome
A new brother, where
Forever you are at home;

And show him
Gravely around yourselves, with
The grand manner of natural powers, like
Weather or myth,

Who stands gravely too
At your threshold, waiting
The almost visible smile,
Your almost visible greeting.

Brigid Her Eve

for Nancy and Conor and a rush Cross

Origins are
Swamps and rush cradles, so never
Mind me if I see
You as no lady but barbarous and
Maybe beautiful, as when
The scurf of winter grass in Galway
Ignites to light or
Rain and you are nothing less
Than metaphor

That I do not care to
Resolve ever and won't ever bother to
Catch close and make small like
Another woman or even
A tower of ivory or house of gold, thus
Missing out on major things like weather
And distances that touch
Other distances right round this
Only and mighty orb

I know the feel of
Up through my legs since
I staggered erect from the
Tremors of trees, in which you
Were a bark skirt and a
Dogbite of roses, most fecund for
A boy lover. And you, do not
Come closer either, for there is
Nothing nearer.

Just simply be;
Continuing, with my own bit
Of history evaporating while
I find big things in consonants, like the
Discovery of a spring well, or
The hunch of a spring plough on the first headland
When all the world was a vowel;
Big things like lost continents;
Something that has your style.

Or lack of style,
Like the raw bulb of the ewe that leaves
A lamb on the green, or the
Tiny earthquake of a snowdrop, nothing
To shake the poles too much, just something
To show you've been around and the day holy
Like Sunday or lucky like
The day when a poet is lucky enough to say
Something of importance to himself

That must
Acknowledge and ignore you, the miracle
Taken for granted, being natural,
As the fields turn over, China
Falling as we come up,
And I stand flatfooted on a slanting land
Content with the old lore, with the womb language
That built you with the sun in a rush
Cross to be hung on every door.

Lost Man In Me

1.

He can forgive
Enormous sins with ease; Hitler at his ear
With the drums of delirium
Not too hard to bear;

Nor the little men that sell out
Neighbour and passion. Inside his tree
Equating leaf and trunk
The big is no more than the moiety,

And the hugest trulls beam
The shy lamps of virgins; on the Petrine rock
The worst popes shine like artifacts;
Not theirs the shepherd's crook

But his for who knows
Who corrupted whom? Not he who stares
At Messalina in the Roman whorehouse
And wholly admires the wares;

And is not too put out when Catherine
Garrots her man. Behind his fan
He listens to Lesbos singing and the voice
Sweet as duet and duel says all that love can:

Which is neither more nor less
Than you, me, sun and moon. He quotes the Hai Ta'u –
'The supreme virtue of heaven is to produce';
And leaves it to me and you,

As if our generals were mere gun
Barrels to a moment that waits upon the trigger.
If any unpin the bomb,
It's in the Thing itself and will it matter?

A round of Yin, then
A round of Yang, that equals the Tao. In
His tree already he forgives them, if
Forgiveness is possible without sin,

As if all
Were turning sweetly on the potter's wheel, the gross
Fungus and the girl about to fall.
The virtue of heaven is simply to produce

Anything. It's a music. Birdsong or bomb
It's all equal. In his Yin-Yang tree
He doesn't ape God but is quite like some
Kind of eternity

In whose paradox I can sing
Who sits in my tree
A million-million years doing nothing
But forgiving me.

2.

Down there, mast high,
He hangs above the world's waters;
Inch after inch he clambers into the sky
On a wincing rope.
This might be the day to die.

One hand holds, one desperate claw
Battered sea-black, green and blue.
The other tears at the canvas gale;
Lurching on a seatop he
Empties the belly of a sail.

Seabooted, unwieldy, wearing no
Wings he should be foundering down
Latitudes that turn to snow;
Instead, he spins
The rough earth on the axis of one toe.

And with a single ropeyarn he
Tugs the hugely blackening west.
The compass in his head is true;
All points at rest.
His bird is married to the sea.

This could be the day. He rolls
Surgewise, seeking it. The shiver
Of water piles up to the Pole.
He jumps the first backstay down,
Spits in a fist, sails on forever.

Lakshmi

A sheet of paper, placed
Over this dangerous bronze figure,
Covers up the East
And the dancer's narrow waist,

India gone, sunken
The archaic shining knot; white paper
Is the churned-up ocean
That casts her upwards, buttocks in motion,

Helmeted hair, enormous
Ear-rings and all, the necklace
In sacred circles; there was
Dancing here that folded into a lotus.

The bare breasts still now, the nubs
At rest, but the twisted rhombs
Of the hips still echo
Temple gongs.

The belly is so young
And the undented navel. Instruments
Should sound like this,
Keeping distance

Like the long arm that falls to the gathering fingers,
Hand sinister, that knows space
Is precious and must not spill.
The two legs are tough with grace –

And since they are the bearers, yield nothing
To immodest silks, who must tower
Up from their native earth
To carry a little flower

Where, coppered above
The heartbeat, on its fine meridian floats
A face flawed with neither age or youth;
Here Ganges pours

But merely rounds the bud
She contemplates, that must not dwindle;
On her right hand it rides, and earth
Turns quietly on the spindle.

Three Houses

1. *Gurteen*

I had no gift for it.
It hung out in the welter of the moor;
A black-faced country staring in

All day. Never did the sun
Explode with flowers in the dark vases
Of the windows. The fall was wrong

And there was uplifted the striking north
Before the door.
We lived in the flintlights of a cavern floor.

It was enemy country too, the rafts of the low
Fields foundering. Every day the latch
Lifted to some catastrophe, such as

A foal dead in an outfield, a calf lost
In a mud-suck, a hen laying wild in the rushes,
A bullock strayed, a goose gone with the fox;

The epic, if any, going on too long.
Nil the glory in it, null the profit;
It was too big for me and full of threat.

A place that glugged green in the vast egg
Of the weather, too littered with rains
And with minor stone-age tragedies like getting wet

Feet in the goose paddock watching
An angel, yes, in the air, in the dusk, taking
A rose petal face out of nothing in particular,

Just happening big out of a glitter,
Unaware of me or the black-avised country where
The half-wheel of the day was bogging down.

Certainly it could have been the moon.
And though I prefer to think otherwise
Nothing happened in the way of ecstasy.

And I took indoors my gawky childhood, still
Unmeasured, through mud and the yard midden
That was acting up and coming into the kitchen

With the milkers, with the men, with the weather,
Feeling as ever that the earth is outside matter
Trying to get in, to get into the very centre

Swamp the sunflowers and stone circles
And all that spirals and wings up, to bring
The tiller back on the old compost heap,

Dung value. Petering out
Like this father-figure at the fire
Crumbling into space, who was something once,

Who was the sage here and the reason, who raised
The roof, begot the tree,
Hedged the apple and built the causeway down

For the postman who never comes, who touched
The harsh sex of the earth that never blooms,
And was gentled by this woman who stands in the door now,

The mistress of a few iron pots,
With the bogface looking in and the barbarous furrows.
I tell of my angel and the bright thing is lost

In the cud of cows, in the farming day,
Never to bloom again and wash the air
Towards Clonkeen Carle. I sit down by the fire

And build my nightly stockade in the ash
With an old catalogue, Army & Navy Stores,
And polish two pennies bright

While earth and day go under. Buoyed up
In their bundles on the nightwave are the plovers,
Blown with the sweet pith of their bones over, the men

Drift off to visit other outposts of
Man in nameless townlands, moon-swollen damps.
The two old people sit it out,

And humped in the very posture of the womb
On a small stool I ride it too,
The dull incessant siege, on the black orb –
The epic, if any, going on too long.

2.   *Shanballard*

It's feeling now and dangerous
To touch, when I
Was the crown prince of birds early
With the first cock crowing;
And that was a morning,
My head pillowed and abroad
In the true blue;
Meaning I felt the world awake
And I was a county.

Meaning up heartwise the house awoke
To the call of a country;
Turfsmoke curled from below
And day creaked open;

Dangling on my rafter I
Survey my kingdom,
Open fire and hanging kettle,
The doorway wide,
The feathered collie in the morning beam.

Meaning the big unsteady dawn was waiting
And world still making,
Meaning the smoking cows halfmade
Wavered on the dews;
And there was a snail humped on a bridge
And there was the blackbird pecked him up
And there was the mare I was to ride
Butting a silly liquid foal.
The day was starting to report.

Meaning it zigzagged off the arrow
Head of a woodcock, meaning it caught crows
Burgling a turnip field, meaning it sat
On the old crowman in the oats,
His crossbow more askew;
Green hung the crabapple claws;
Rabbits announced me, here
Comes Twolegs and his totem dog;
The thumped morse went on before me.

Meaning it went up into the breath
Of morning, meaning I bowed before
The bowlegged blackthorn in the gap
Where the sunburst met me.
And I was the bogvoice going up,
I was the beginning bees,
I was the dialogue in the curlew's mouth
And simple as a two-holed pipe;
The ripe fern turning south.

Meaning the sun was sailing me, and all
The call of crows on Lynch's knoll was mine;
And lying down I was
The newest butterfly white and green
Drying its wayward compass on a stone,
And the all around and the all to be
Turning over

To catch the three small chimneys on the hill
Treadling the morning smoke.

Meaning the cat loped after the milker
And swallows chuckled
On the byre beams above the cans, meaning
Pigs sang at the sty gate,
And two old men,
Two lovely raggedly old men gossiped
By the upheeled cart, and morning
Was over, done, gone, and never
To be followed after;

Meaning I,
Catching the sun upon a breakfast knife,
No longer beamed;
Housed I was and never homed again,
A dwindled fellow.
Folded the buzzing miles outside the pane
Where the drunken gatepost leaned
And a single foxglove rolled its bells around
A stick tall as an umbrella.

3. *Knockroe*

The river god sat down
In Summer pools. The Satyrs or their male
Correlatives in Gaelic haunted
Bankside and haycock:
It was that season of the year.

Even the sun searched for the female form.
The dayscreen was hers, night flitted
As if from a halfmoon before her;
Her dayshift over,
She lived upon the scandals of the night.

I was the wooded brute then on the road,
Horns in the night bush. Unlimited
The fight, the free-for-all; no
Woman could cover that
Amount of country, so the country did it,

And blocked her out in capitals of trees
On hills and tapped the air
For delicate lights, as I for words. It went
Hard with me
In the old Landleaguer's house,

Dowsing the summer's water, raking hay,
Handling a horse or footing next winter's turf
Yet it went gay with me who thought
She must be there, be here,
Would come, would come, all things being right,

Who heard the old men talk, the old men say
Something that belonged to her and me,
Land war or cattle stir, some small
Epic with a lift
Was a tall heroic body we could share,

Shining, one to the other, two top
People with a need for deeds. I trained
Tough for something that would never happen,
But happened daily
And ever would happen, being simply me.

Come you now and take the words that make you,
Oblivious twin, all woman, my one peer;
My dark, my darling, full of rage and grace,
Come, Goddess,
Of all your faces show me just one face.

Sunday Morning

*   If I make way for bells on Sunday morning,
    Demure, deep in
    Her Sunday hat she'll walk, tipping the tall
    Flowering shrub, a lilac, at
    The corner
    Turning into Mespil Road.

A street new from the font, an old
Arrow of canal
Mounted, tufted by an ancient swan, is leading
Somewhere;
My bible woman hardly knows
The way she goes.

She carries the total injury of me;
In jeopardy. Almost
Rural the scene with elm and planetree, sun
At summer hoist, a wisp
Of smoke from some pedestrian;
Her penitent feet will lead her on.

She does not dally by the sluice
Or the resting barge. An odd head
Hangs on the bridge at Baggot Street;
God is dead,
His shadow what I throw for
Beyond into hurt and metaphor.

The whole world can see the lover's hands
Upon her. In the din
Of sweet bells she rises to confess
The evil bruise;
Hears another gospel start
In the regions of the heart;

What penitence can she profess?
How burn away
Back into her first
Girl-smile
The garden fallen around her, simple trees,
Lovers and enemies?

Brother Twin

One lagging his old bones
Against the winter wind in Connacht
Herds sheep and listens
To the other side:
'The Bodhisattva Manjusri
Is the master of transcendental wisdom'.

The other, shaven twin
In the empty begging bowl of the East,
Wakens on a stupa, the holy dead forgotten,
Saying: 'The soft West
Is arriving on the sheepwalks, tomorrow
The lactation of ewes'.

The ram's groom relaying the fertile thing
Dies for a moment, new grass
Forgotten, showery Phallus
No weather king:
'The fifth station is that of a Bodhisattva,
No turning back'.

In the famine yawns the saintly twin:
'Nothing dies, not even
Man's dream of woman;
All night she walks, the honey drips, the sky
Is one great eye. In Galway now
A girl destroys infinity'.

Flushed from the female, turning over, brother
Sings to his opposite: 'Outrageously
Made of seven precious substances
Is the Bodhi-tree;
And they squat there accomplishing each sign,
Manjusri as Manjughosha on a lion,

Buddhas beyond recall, their
Dialogue done.
Hang up the skeleton. What chores delight us?
What women intervene?'
Manjusri's attributes are book and sword:
His too the tall blue lotus.

Trevaylor

First, this
Prayer, that you the people
Gone over, ghosts, bright
Narcissi, lean into my pool now
And be this poem.

Empty are
All mirrors you do not countenance;
The fabulous water is
Fathomed by no horizons
Till you come, till you appear.

I offer you
Only the barest stems. Sunflowers,
Come! Gather your lives
About me here. People
Me in those local airs

Which were yours, which
Are you, which
I breathe. Your flaws over me.
Let them rise and ruffle,
The colours rich

So that I have
Dimensions beyond me, where
You are form and dimension. Tread my
Mirror hugely, people,
That the great thing appear.

Painting of My Father

1.

I saw him to the last, the grey
Casting of the face,
The crabbled hands like this
Yielding to the cluster of the Rosary;

I who barbered you occasionally
And filled your pipe
Dropping into your deafness the odd item
Of family news that never
Exactly reached you,

For you were away already.

So your true going was a sort
Of mutual release. 'Lord', you whispered hanging
That day in my arms naked
As Jesus down from the cross,
'Take me away'.

Now for me this vague distress
And a guilt that grows;
What is it that one owes a father?

And cannot pay,

Liaison lost with the broad
Dialect of the child where words
Were the throbs of a countryside

Big like a sheepshearing or small
As the lark pinned high above
The water meadows where we drank our tea,
The trout waiting in the fishing river;

Eternal precincts
Of a huge present tense, as if
You were not due to be left
Abandoned like an old
Settlement;
The young being
Unscrupulous in their growing up.

So you wanted little of me towards the end,
Barbering, a light
For the old pipe,
And an ear, my ear, any ear, when you spilled over
The intolerable burden
Of being a very old man.

2.

An image that wounds;
Better even
The figure of power, the
All father,
Jahwah, Helios or another; not
That I'd like you in big translations
Who were rich enough
As your own man.

For you were daylight's own fellow and over
The moonsuck of the mother
All male and master under heaven;
And that's how you come into mind,
In taut middle-age when you were quite
The masher,
Velvet collar, tan velour
Overcoat, plush hat and handmade boot,
In those streets round the cattlemarket where
Our evenings were a summer saunter;

Hanlon's Corner, Stoneybatter,
The Broadstone, MGWR
Where trains run no more,

And I half expect round any corner
The hastening dandy, country
Things still clinging;
Blue the gaze;
Delicate the gait, the dancer,
Angler, fowler, hurler, football player;

Tomorrow
Formally as a bullfighter he'll pace
The horned pens and the cattle slobber,
Face the loss or net the profit
Stonily
As befits the gambler;

And at noon lean
Recomposed on the railed wall
By the City Arms, yarning, true Ulyssean,
Over a shoe shine.

And now here
Above the walnut desk, the only familiar in
This strange hallucinatory land I found
Late, you stare out; again
All age, all pain, at the very end
Of your long span: not you indeed
But every man;
Just waiting.

Land's End some few miles away; the tide
Is white round the mount; a bird
Stands on the sundial on the lawn; Spring
Is hovering;
And in the tulip tree – hallucination – some
Medieval person reads a tome

(To disappear battered
By a rainshower with his
Monkshood, creature of air;
The bird stays on, real enough;
A woodpecker)

A country ironed out
Into saints and menhirs where
You never put a foot,

Where the weather camps for an hour before
It stamps the soft shires, taking over
The whole south of England at a blow.

Curragh, November Meeting

Distances are
Threaded over, a web. And the same spider
Spins the tale of
The dying sun.

Caught on his last legs. Bleaching too
Are the bright horses: jackets
And jockeys run
Out of pigment, are

A caveman's scratches, a jostling script.
There's some time left
To use your magic on it, wish
The winner home

Down Walsh's hill into
The drumbeat of the straight. Here
We go offering
The thing a heart, the spectacle a home:

And half ashamed of it, the child's
Play, the toys in colour now
Thumping their own life out of us, galloping
Into the heart

And away. Gone. Tomorrow the
Empty stands, the moneyspinner in
His winter coat;
And all forgotten.
                    Nomads no more

It means nothing, nor should; a mock-up
Since we dropped that wild pulse settling down at last,
Suburban fathers: or at most a slight
Affair with a trumpet blast.

Athenry

1.

The guidebook gives it date and dignity;
And disengages me. The place is alien.
Though I've rubbed raw against the geography
The heartbeat here's not mine;
Simply dead history.

Norman, it says, original walls; meaning
Those old stone wounds and moon mends,
Watch-towers gone native into
Treetops and birds' nests
Where I wished up the watching country

And purely civilian wagged with the daws
My early cradle, the warman
Dispersed among the thousand names of grass;
Honey is on the spike;
The golden skulls fall to the beekeeper.

I disown them, the masters and
The lordly Abbots greedy for heaven who holed up
Here in the very thigh of Christ,
I mean in the tumbled chancel where the East
Hangs crucified on one great Abbey window

And on a strut of stone I rode the beam
Of morning sometime I can't remember,
Ten townlands in my breath;
And truly a grassman with no history
Trod on every hill,

Rueveha, Raheen, Esker, Mountbawn, do
My footprints show
Where my fathers loom green into the blue
Hills of Roxborough?
How young I am in the plain of the bird's eye.

2.

Notable for its cattle fairs, says the book.
Follow me here. I am
The Antlered boy,
A wood of horns my home. I move
Where great beasts in the street rise out of mud:

I go forth in a caul of dung. I
Am at home in the house of the people,
Their genuflections are mine,
Mine the Barbaroi with the green thumbs,
Cousins on the one dug.

Mark how this fair morning the very earth
Arrives on the doorstep, men
Who are wedges of weather, who will depart
On footprints of stubble, leaving
The dark down on the day.

And a void that the mud fills, leaving
A mess; and as ever it's raining:
There's a cart abandoned at the town's end;
Casualties dribble in the pubs;
And my limping uncle's on the booze again;

I cry for the lift of the morning, whose clay feet
Are mud melting
Into that old drunk from Derrydonnel
Always the last and maudlin in the night
To home on his distant candle light;

Ass-eared and tumbrilled, with his silent wife
He'll arrive; unlike me left
Wilting with the time, I
In the morse
Hoofbeats of the horse,

The jargon of the Gods maybe, and maybe
I tuned in on some heraldic thing:
(Erect me a monument of broken wings)
However divine the arguments
I lost them every one

And am so vulnerable I stand here now
At a town's edge shying
Away from some old misery. Quem tu, quem tu,
Melpomene . . . . A fellow out of character
In any room but a field

Who wept at school, that whole first month,
For the great Inadequate left after
Where myth becomes fear,
Careful lest a living odour leak from the creature,
And the dog dig up Caesar.

The Small Town of John Coan (2)

1.   Remand

Sailing the last date out and away
Beyond birthdays on face perhaps
May distract him from
Such infinities

As there are; a gaze,
Hardly a girl yet, pupped between two
Furloughs from Flanders Field;

She rose out of it with white paps
Aching so young they heaped his
Hands full.
           What happened
To the doll face that brought to the half-doors
The town spinsters where on propped up

Elbows they waited for time to round the tale,
Snake and apple fall?

2.   Maud Gonne

In a Noh play she
Would be the heartbeat left
To some famous numinous name straddling
Haunted centuries of highway,

A passionate body caught
Between worlds in an endless jet
Of feeling, for whom the final death is not;

A silhouette
I keep seeking, remembering how an old
Shawled slum-body was transfigured on
The Metal Bridge one winter sunset

Walking out of the rose
Visored and greaved, in whole barbaric gold,
Bellona, War's own maiden, no simpering poet's Muse.

3.   *Genius Loci*

Unthinking youth had sparked and fizzled to
The unceasing woman, yet never struck fire really
Till he was the sober pew, the settled piece
Of family furniture.
              And then but the once
And only for a moment did earth roll back, the stone
Turn;
                For a tinker Moll, absurdly garbed
In trailing handmedowns, in purple, on a ditch,
The tents behind her and all Tartary.

The conflagration was dowsed decently,
The bog road and the blue sat steady down,
Space filled up.

              But there's a want
In every daylight since, a wayside place
Stretched to the limits with the savage face
Of the brute goddess its inhabitant.

4.   *Encounter*

And I on the Alley Bridge
Unjointing the rod that evening, summer
Aloft and slow and
All the old ones out in Abbey Row

When behind me up she rears
In her daffodil jumper, her
Whoring number; and she peers into my fishbasket
Low, low.

Pisces two.
            Some are dead
Who mumbled into her buttercups, gone down
The darling men, the King's very own.

And still it's on offer, that very ardent lap,
Though it's said the battered elm in Leonard's lawn,
The lover's tree, has even got the clap.

5. *Heureux Qui Comme Ulysse*

Over the smother of the rain
His mother with a violin hung out of heaven;
La donna e mobile;

He answered her, spreadeagled on
The crutch of his own instrument, his face
In the buttend of a candle; rapt I suppose away.

That was in the bakehouse twenty years ago
When it was a melody –
              I mean Time
When it was his galleon, scrolled wind, hefted numen;
O Jesus what guttered on the puddle?
                     Dough in trow and bin
Waiting the morrow, the oven, the reality.

                   He doesn't know
He'll leave too late, come back broken, sit
Over the trickling street on a sack of bran
With a foul pipe.
               No-man.

6.

She'd thumbed her way from the source
Of every faery story, simply
Taking his over; a nudity
On a white horse.

At least that's what he'd like to tell;
Actually it fell
Out differently of course.

There was a horse all right, a fat pad
On which she
Our beauty rode

Spangled and pirouetting over the mud
And sawdust of Taylor's field, a circus ride.
He was aged six but that was the night
On which he was destroyed.

7.

Sometimes I'd like to write: 'Dear Helen,
Admit me no more
Into the epic by
The back door.'

Like last night when I froze
In the yard with a barrel of rainwater,
A spy – I'd sunk that low –
On her new visitor.

Candle, glim, or blued lamp,
O great God in Heaven that
He should heap with light that ample rump
While the sky turned on my table and it grew late;

And she let him out where I coped with the night chills,
A freakish lad with wings on his heels.

8.

Comment: when the bare
Triteness of age hums
With old Gospel words, when his deeds
Are nil and his needs nulled, ten to one she comes
Making a final last appearance;

Never like this
In a fieldway holding
The heliograph of a daisy head.

God
Be good to this lover. He watched her become
Too loud a music for the room
No matter the hand on the piano, his
Least of all in consequence,
He earned his peace,
Breaking, being no glass to rise and fall
Intermittently to every squall.

9

He'll come back, stand exactly here –
Footprints never blow away like leaves –
Above him the same crows sawing;
It's spring always under the rampart trees.

He'll say: 'Time was when heaven loved a child'.
And for a simple moment that's what he believes;
And believes for a moment a world grown mild;

And perhaps pick up as before the same skyblue
Crow's egg unharmed and whole
From its tree fall.

Holding it the large unaching earth is true,
Forever the uttering birds, the leafy boy
Scored in the dapple, his small footprints
In the midst of great improbable events.

10.

Clubbed by the evening bell
From the roughcast tower in goes the earlier man
To candle dip and soft shoes,
White surplice, black soutane.

He moves the holy place into the beam;
Now the westering south gives room
She rides in on a piece of glass,
A face more told than any tale.
                     The several
Pious souls inhabiting the aisle
Will never know his thurible is aimed
Beyond them, how maimed he is

Who watches the red wick in the colza oil;
Too mothered.
                     Always fronting him
Veronica holding out a towel.

11.

He puts back on his severed head
And a town trite as a platitude
Offers him his face in blood;

And sings so sweetly with his mouth
The hurts of youth;

As if what lives – where suppurates
The history that has no dates –
Were bidding him lift up his head
Transfigured with neurotic dread

And listen to it giving tongue
Sweet as Solomon his song
For the young;

And all the sweeter for the art
Of the thorn in his heart.

12.

Delicate
The sensual skin of our town; tap
A gable and the timbrel
Of a person answers;

Such a stuff, not stone, not timber,
Simply a state
Of being there, living the similar,
Or sharing a space

Or a common psyche, puffed large
Into the variable of the weather,
In which each one secretly
Seeks selfish some sodden glory.

But if one sins all fall. There's no assent
Yet the town twangs like an instrument.

Summer and a liquid bird
In the high stones: a tower
In a garden is something, like a sword
Upstairs.

But towers have lived so long
The gods have annexed them: in each a lover
Mailed and clinking yields to the dulcimer:
Mars is taken by a song.

Who mentioned Elenore?

A baker in a paper hat
Relieves himself against the rampart wall;
Over the privet blows an apple.

What would she dare
Here in the huge descending West? What troubadour
Would gild her scandals, offer her
Golden ball, golden sandals?

Heroes 1916

Occasionally talking
Of cities seen,
not from a wave-top in
A mother of pearl morning, showering spires
Left over by the gods,
but other, the dream was other, and

I watched them, common men, fall back
Into place, the big rhythms
Peeling off,
soon to sit
Shabby, wingless, on grass heels, between
The turnip drills

And heroes must die
On their feet, in their own
Enormous footprints, out there on the sky,
Each man unique, and man alone,

Not gossiping
Of cities seen in
The passing smoke,

Birmingham, Coventry, Liverpool,

Their day done.

Lakshmi

Last night nothing, no blink
At the crossroads. And this morning the down
Sky – as if something
Had happened I should have known;

Leaving me dumped
On an unkempt Sunday, making
A chore of the light. What is it
This lump of clay, this I, has failed to see?

Come up with it.
What am I without a happening?
You are the event, the uncertain
Constant,

And difficult, lotus,
The marvellous stillness in the pool,
The crown jewel in the well.
And you can be so small,

A tiny symbol, like
A fern leaf in the hand, that opens
Out of a silver ball, uncurls
In a silver abstract the great tree of the heavens

That fits
Into the veins, bears the body, suits
The infinite, consoles
Not a soul but simply waits

The moment that displaces
The usual earth; like this poem I
Turn inward after you
And the many secret faces

You leave life after life to
Flow into one, some unity
Like you or
The fabulous tree.

So whatever moved
Into station last night, Goddess, leave
Bright for me to circle
With the gravity of a satellite.

A Certain Person

Ten foot high is a lord;
Pallas Athene, give me
My portion now that I'm tired,
And a little man as a toady,

A certain plum-coloured codger,
And let him make me suit;
A little bum-wagging dodger
Of the third sex, and a tout;

One who's thrived on the flavour
Of lickspittle or worse,
An obscene jaunt whose saviour
Jingles in his purse;

A trull, a doll, a livery,
The smell of the Fall on his face;
A ludicrous little flunkey
Who stands between me and grace,

Stands ten foot high in his lord,
The money-changer; I say
I'm tired, lady, I'm tired,
For the traffic is all his way;

Osiris who weighs all souls
Sat poets high on a feather,
But this lout's fouled the controls
And we're back to the shoe leather;

He walks the town unloved,
Yet sits down everywhere,
A footboy once removed
Who's sneaked up stair by stair.

All I ask, Good Lady,
Is to pull off the ten-foot socks,
Sever the head from the body
And the jungle from the money box

And scatter the pieces fairly
Where they came from, where he crawls
Out in the scrawled graffiti
Of the moon in urinals.

Body

I'll wear it out perhaps
To a suit of wrinkle, a skin
Too large
With the soul shrinking;

The will gone out of it,
Yet all the daily rent to pay;
Flesh that cannot last,
Soul that never got under way:

Too much houseroom now;
Tomorrow none;
But paying either way
For journey done, for journey not begun.

A Bit of Brass

A horn hung on an oak;
And he, the big overplus, the hero
Destined, sounds the famous note, invokes
Cascading Gods and
His own death boat.

I did lift
A bit of battered brass once to my mouth,
May 1915, after
A day's rain
In the townwalled field where the Volunteers
Drilled;

That evening the wet overhang had daunted all,
Bugler and mate
Gossiped under a leaking branch, sounding
An occasional call,
Joe Egan, Josie Rooney;
Dear Posterity, I was there.

Echoes hung
Solidly in the drowned green beechtrees,
Hardly swinging;
Call after call brought no one to the field,
That is no man alive;
The mates gave up and I purloined the thing;

Squawk, a couple of fancy tootles,
Then out of Me minus
It came, the soaring
Thing;
Just once.

It could be it still hangs
In the May over
Leonards and the Pound Walk, just waiting
Those fellows, the long striders
Gods or men
To take the field.

Duddy's Wall

Mon semblable in
Tattered velvet, battered sandals, dangling
From his five years over
The goings on in Duddy's Livery Yard

Half morning has
Died on the sundial, the other half
Is the giant's eye on my forehead
Seeing everything

That happens, such as T. Heavey, Saddler,
Clambering over the Rampart wall to
Loosen his belt;
And a strawman in Shaughnessy's stack

Tilting at an old cow, eternal
Dragon of the gardens; and there's the Regan girl
Hobbled in red flannel pegging out
Her drawers:

Which facts I record, noting
At the same time how the rooks
Chuckle just outside my halo; world comes
Also over the treetops where the sky is

Moving in peaceful parables; not that
My geography goes round the sun, I am
The nub middle, sit, squat
On my stone butt surveying

One Mike Delaney, Ostler, in the echoes
Below me, talking guttersnipe
To a sad angled gearraun
Called Charley

Harnessing up, and a Duddy (Tommy) with
A barrow of new dung, both
Steaming, while Tom the Father
Beard and all comes following after

Leading another unarching bit of horseflesh
Fully caparisoned
For a funeral walk. Berny
Quinn is dead, poor man:

Clay pipes for every manjack mourner,
Snuff in saucers
For the weeping world on the kitchen board;
Already the bellringer's in the loft

And the family ghosts
Pleading for decent burial, reminding me –
Who digs the hole
For Berny Quinn, son of the carpenter?

Once I saw him topple in a fit.
Now this day is his, we follow him
Around two streets; proud heroes strut
For one perched high, tophatted, one Michael Delaney, mute.

(Who doesn't know as
He fly-flicks daintily one big gelding's ear,
How soon himself must go,
And how much further

Past the old tower undone
As a headless Knight, and into the fable
Of the fall-down Abbey.
Of a red haemorrhage on Duddy's table)

And that was a day in my fathering fellow,
First Adam, pre-fall,
Scuffing with a toe the planetary surface
On Duddy's wall.

The Skellig Way

The March crow furnishes his twig
In the knowledge that a bigger bird
Above the blow
Is hatching out the whole raw yolk of spring.

There's no Lent in the twitching rookery;
Pair by pair they go,
Feather to feather married;
Easter the nodal point in earth's revolution.

Listen, you dumb stone faces to the West,
You on Skellig Michael,
White hoods of God,
Hermits abounding in the unseen graces,

Matins, and Lauds and Vespers are sung here
In a loud vernacular
Above the trees;
Can you do better down on your knees?

Three Poems

1.

Only here if
I look for them one sauntering forth
In her black shawl or
Pinned to the doorway with the long street
To one eye like a telescope;

The other just a face
Floating in the turnsmoke within;
She was the saint, hobnobbing with the greater galaxies,
Taking credit accordingly
When I passed examinations.

I love them now who never
Saw them really, or unwillingly: days
They look out of windy November with
The chimneys in a smudge
Of illiterate initials all down the street,

Alive, the darlings, in a sort of love for me;
Penury's hangovers, yet
How they'd hate this, to be the poor
Relations to a poem, tugged forth from
Their decent anonymity;

Bridget and Delia, spinsters deceased;
Tom brother, the breadwinner, carrying the can,
In the Temperance Hall the Parliamentarian,
And Michael the dandy with the highbred look of hunger
And the delicate impossible languor.

Too late I want to know them now,
Like God a lover, who must share with them forever
This furrow of a street
Full of the ghostly bloom
Of dead semen.

2.

Beside them that lightfoot wife,
Stone barren,
Who drifted towards the hornmad in the way
The moon sinks
A well in every water drop.

And I wonder, outside charity, what image
Of love she begat in them
Who watched her, the Who's Who
Of town lovers,
Corrupting the nightwatch and the family rosary:

Barren naturally; then –
Hallucinated Jesus – to grow round as a plant pot
In the parlour window!
To shake it out, the blessed blossom, like
The very mother of God, in the chapel aisle,
Sunday's woman!

What invisible lover beaked her nape, to be
After forty years in fruit, adding
The unbearable mystery of fatherhood?

As if, in a chagrin of virgins, some new thing was mooting
Like a dispensation; Moses
Down from the barbarous rock-face, still
Shaking with rainbows.

3.

I'd like to assure myself I really saw her
The new girl,
Walking down the street the first day,

And not borrowed her from the poet
Of another wobbly old town, that died
Three thousand years ago,

That offered to the summer evening a like
Paraphernalia, old men on the sills,
Iron ringing in a forge.

I cannot recollect if I was rolling a hoop
Or playing with the taus
When I heard the new silence and discovered her

Passing on the bare uncobbled way, leaving
An Iliad behind,
Just liberating the one line

That grows and grows into resonance, as if
She touched him in passing,
The old man of Chios, who was blind,

Who needed only the whisper of her sandal
To set the topless towers on fire,
Consuming incidentally all women else,

So that it hurts me to try to remember
How much I remember of a face that's disappeared
Nameless in the glory of another.

Yesterday's Man

I sit staring
At the old notebook. And that was the year
That never, I thought, rose off the ground,
The dull one, nose to the grindstone,
Unabashed by lack of wing:

Yet here, confronting me
With an air of great doings, is an old familiar
Still edged and luminous with
Its ache towards infinity, striving
Out of the very mortality of my parts

To strike the attitudes of (circa) 1480
Pico, Ficino, of Florence, Platonists
In love with their own divinity (like me,
Apotheosis round the corner
Sometimes on good days)

Quotations, pages of them, from the wrong men
Naming the Gods with new jubilance,
Going tandem on the paradox.
'Let us enter' says Pico, 'into the light of ignorance';
'Blindness', says another, 'is the inspiration of the eye!'

And madness more than sanity. Somewhere
The Blessed sit drunken to an eternal feast.
Who but Venus and Minerva crowns the Faun
Blessed with annihilation pouring forth
His dithyrambs, enigmas of Blind Love?
And why does all this rubbish chime with me

Who see soberly the orgy die?
Where was I going on a gust like that? And so
Much trivia round, the daily stuff,
Appointments, people forgotten, a neat row
Of telephone numbers empty now
As any bombed-out terrace in the town:

Lines of verse too left littering
After poems that never got underway.
A pen drawing, very odd, the Storm God Zu
Trussed in his fowl form to a carrying pole;
(From him the wren-walk on St. Stephen's Day)

Copied, I suppose, to prove a point,
(Akkadian seal, Babylonian cylinder?) How
Much at home I am in this mad world
Suddenly and again! And here somewhere
You the girl enter

Anonymously, in two wooden stanzas, into which
You have entirely disappeared. Words, words,
That's all you are, girl who never
Was a lover. And I likened you,
Body I could see through, to a catapult

Pulled tight and launching;
(Pinching shamelessly another poet's image)
But also to a hill pipe, as if your flesh was lost
To the air. Amor, amor,
Where has love gone from the cry of old men

That I have to imagine you afresh, as if
I sat there in the Custom House window over
The salt harbour, a young man?
And is it really better
To rage than remain aloof and

Ignore you, never again to
Relearn the resonances? Amor modus
Perpetuus et copula mundi. The
Magnificence, Proclus, Iamblichus, Porphyry,
And the nonsense.

Ambiguous territory for the halt and lame.
Wounds bleed forever. Move on before
A red heart shakes the bone structure. Here is
Excerpt and excerpt. 'Eros jouant avec
Un Masque de Sileni'. Now where did I get that?

And Venus as a Mater dolorosa!
'Not milk', she says, 'do you suck, O savage child,
But the tears of things'. And, my God, Theocritus –
Love and Death exchanging arrows, young
Men die and old men fall in love.

No decorum in the universe.
Sit in the draught, old Body, dream away
And between stumbles make your bit of verse:
No decorum in the universe,
That's what I say

Closing the diary of yesterday's man.
The bay blues the eye; below
Wages a quayside memory, the Frau
Of the Dutch Captain's hanging out her wash,
So young, so young, transfiguring me.

A Tribal Digression

The last man left,
His frieze fellows vanished with their sheepcrooks and carts
Into the blue, the sheepfair
Truly over,
And still he dallies in Nolan's or Glynn's,
Horse and creel at the door;

It's a full nightfall,
With the lunatic old beard in drunken never-ending
Spate, his wife from the starlight
Leaning in, whispering
From her peaceful shawl the odd
Appeasing word.

But I know that stone head.
Never, never will there be peace in it, and though I share
The House of the people with him I
Have not forgotten
An older inhabitant, the shocker with
The savage stare

Shaking a stone axe over
A spoil of ewes. Who says that country knees go down
To any shored-up Christ
Or the soft sylvan deity of the Fellahin
Standing in stubble fields listening
To the wounded grain?

Here's warrior caste,
Ambushed lord and bludgeoned cattledrive, no ruth,
No green man with
An ivy cock for Sunday,
In some stratum one with me and all the incalculable
Hysterias of unbonded man.

In God's own time he'll climb into his creel,
Wife beside him, silent soul:
Not far to go,
Zigzagging between Bootes and the Agricultural
Experimental Station, two
Miles out the Galway Road.

Name Plate

for Helen

My name plate is
Largely outsize, and since it was presented to me
The night I was born by
An unknown woman, something of a mystery

Who saw her at my cradle side
I don't remember. There were no strangers in town,
No circus or penny gaff,
No one, indeed, unaccounted for, yet here she was

Leaning over me with a glitter
Out of her January fur, and this thing in her hand;
Good fairy, said my mother
Later, and promptly decided I'd make a Doctor,

Or a Vet or a Dentist, even a Solicitor
My titles on lasting brass;
And I never gave it a thought, just soldiering on
Nameless, almost anonymous; now and then

Plagued by the vision of a woman leaning over me
Holding out this bit of raw silver
That disappeared in the moonlight, leaving
A most extraordinary nudity.

Argo

1.

The fleece drew them, a famous
Rainmaker, garment of a God, far off, far off;

And golden too
Where it hung on
The mysterious tree, with a dragon on sentry-go;

And they swarmed over me, adventurers,
Half-winged fellows with gods' names and
Famous bucklers
Who sat, ate, drank and inhabited me
While I became world

And rode all water whole
As a dolphin

2.

My sin was to become delicate,
To shine, to glow, to become
Honey-skinned,
To recite my name, to enumerate my qualities,
Babbling like any hero.

Argus my maker stood upon the tilt
Of my swan prow. This is not my work, said he.
This was a human
Ache towards majesty.

Harshly he stamped me to the sea-top,
I responded singing
Like a harp.

And Jason said, the vessel now is mine
It has filched a body and turned
Itself into my quest.

And that night we lay-to near an island,
And women came aboard me
Fornicating on the corpses
Of dead men.

3.

How many they were, those half- and quarter-blooded thrusters?
Just one to me;
(All Gods are one eventually)

I was the One, mark that; it was I
Outrode the clashing cliffs, outranged the singing rocks,
Lacking respect, outraging
The proper deities.

Whose iron but mine welded the death
Of good King Cyzicus?

Who danced with Rhea till she wedded me
In well water
And had some lover image of me cast
From an old wine stock, calling the thing
Jason, Jason,
Weeping after me
                    (who had form after form now to use)
Who was Hylas, a water-glass, and Polydeuces,
Who was Butus whose stock still thrive,
To honey helmets, who was so many people, so many things,
So many places,
And still lives

If only to remember one face,
A maid's.

Who even as I was alone for the first time
Fronting the brazen bulls

(Myself, only myself then, simply
The boy-man Jason) came to me saying,
The way to their hearts,
Is by way of my love;

Speaking to one without pith,
Whose substance was melting into the earth;
Maid, I said, it is life I love at this moment.
Who replied, I am your life.

So that I ceased to see the snorting smoke of
The beasts before me,
And yoked them, tackled them to the plough
And sowed the terrible seed provided by
Goddess Athena,

Men, armed men, she sprang up
In the furrows behind me,
Who waited me in phalanx;
Who delivered me
From them

By tossing into their midst
A stone quoit,
Which they fought for, destroying one another to the
Last man.

I was content then to let things lie,
Forget fleece, forget the gods semi and demi, heroes
And kings, for there was this maid's face
Staring me from the great white staring world;
Now, she said, it is the question of the dragon.

This, she said, is a labour for you alone.
It is what you must offer for
My maidenhood.

Was it difficult,
Hard, strenuous, bloodletting? was the issue
In doubt, to the very last in doubt,
Was I, Argo, almost overcome?

Certainly not,
            For this time I was all
The heavenly tribe who'd ridden me over the wavetops;
I was fifty
Bolts in one.
The clash was enormous.

Later the signs would be notable and remarked
A leak where some
Good heart shed blood,
A plank missing a limb, a sail short
Of a raven primary.
Trifling injuries but
They brought me to bed,

Here, honoured for a season at
So much a head (Children free) while I
Wept the salt away

Arriving at last on the mud up-creek
Withering away
To the one real and loving thing in me,
The maid's face
Who fell to the fool that I ennobled for a day.

They called him Jason.

And I wonder how they lived, and if
It was happy ever after,
What family they had, et cetera,
Et cetera....

Envying their mutual joy
In one another,
Their mutual laughter.

Argo Left

Up river, silting over, dies
The crestfallen craft, the global outrigger
Shelved and forgotten,
Concerned no more with large affairs
In this world or another;

And no one knows exactly where.
The shag can perch upon a wooden head
Rotting slowly
That once upon a time was rampant god
And no accomplice to mere matter.

This sailor had its living furniture,
Heroes in trim,
Before the flag died on the flagstaff and
The sea forgot to swim
And the rainbow went back into the water.

Friends, what happened? Is the halo of the martyr
No headgear for a man?
Will nobody carry on, be blind
And deaf to all save a mad prompting when
The reason for the trumpets lies behind?

Some Land War Casualties

1.

The one, even with her autumn sheaf, could light
Up with sudden gifts: the other,
Carved up for some pious stoup, was merely
Passing through; dear Elder Brother
Inhabited the leather armchair:
And there were three

In Cross Street, in that cutstone terrace
Notable, caved up inside
A fancy window that was rodded over
With tinted beads.

A French clock that was grandmother's:
And a small annuity perhaps.

2.

Sunday the horde of country shawls. Do I
Remember them, ladies two, the hushed aisle,
The dove on the altar,
One walking wooden up a bright-niched sky
To be happy ever after?
But Maudlin my darling, journey never done,
Spun of my own gossamer, is still and
With that bright hat forever sailing on.

3.

Certainly I remember Mr. Davis,
Cape, leather anklets, deerstalker, the double
Barrel marching down our street:

The winter's laid a cold linoleum down,
Fully appointed bearded Edward Rex
Steps forth in delicate iambics

Gently at the town's end to let wind
And, gun forgotten, belch
Not even rancorously towards Galway.

And I
Cannot remember why when how or if they
Were split by death or swept away
As one in the great 'Flu.
                              A family
That left no murmur or memory,
Their tablets me.

Dardanelles 1916

Last night in stomped
Our Connaught Ranger, Private Patrick Carty
On his way:
        Fully accoutred now, a ramp
Of belts and bandoliers, a bayonet
Wags at his side with no wound yet, the heavy
Haversack sits high:

        Filling the back kitchen, squinting
Down from the roofbeams, shyly
Shaking hands all round the family, smiling;
Me he picks up and by God kisses me.

        Up there under
The brown-white plaster an unknown soldier's face
Is weeping.

        Do I remember more? The urchin daughters
Bold for once and peeping
Washed and ribboned through the door to wave
Him off on the Mail, the 4.15, and away
Where muted now in a long sand he lies, if not
Entirely melted into
The steadfast bony glare of Asia Minor.

One Easter Morning

The first Ephebe thunderstruck between
The maidenhead and the mother sweats with fear:
Narcissus drops eternal anchor here,
The swathed genital the dangerous theme;

Already he carries the thousand years of me,
My broken nakedness, my old-age cry;
And I the lonely terror of the boy,
Unable for Mother Ogre and the mystery.

In between are the lover's years. Forgive
The time that never found the clockfaced moon
Chime with the moment that brings us two alive,

That brings to love the fabulous young head
And love's own body to an ageing man,
To you the gold shower and the vast untrammelled bed.

Encounter At Penshurst

To come by her thus, by accident,
In the Sidney bailiwick, in apple Kent,
And be taken

In her happening, in the old man-pull;
Witch, in her meridian, sitting under
The Greenwich tree,

Gold, russet, she was luminous they say;
And here but a very small bronze
Death mask, beaked as a prow

Where shamelessly aquiver I hang
Over a queen, baited by the
Tiny Eidolon,

Sinking towards the mouth with all
Those earls and groomsmen, jostling for room –
At a lover's height there is no death

But one face in the ecliptic. (Some
Necrophilia certainly.) I do
Commune in some love act

With her sailing island perhaps, its Drakes and drums
Forgetting the railing shrew
For the narrow stomacher, the woman's writ in the red hair,

Even the old royal raddled idol wishing England up
Out on the galleoned seas into
The new geography.

A Hedge Schoolmaster

Any niche is my college.
In wayside ditch roofed by a bramble
I light the small rush candle
Of knowledge in numbskulls.

No mouth-open fledglings sit
Around this Socrates on the turf
But Pat's famished son, the lout
And his daughter, scrapings of the pot.

Thankless the task, to create
Fine manners on salt and potatoes,
To hatch out the morrow's priest
From father's old waistcoat;

Spelling out for the shockhaired
The wars of Caesar,
Hannibal in the Alps or
The Emperor Nero on the fiddle;

To construct with a slate pencil the town of Troy,
Thumbnailing the geography of heroes;
All history from Adam down
To hobble home on bare toes;

With profit and loss and mensuration
Goes towering Agamemnon
And Arius with his heresy
Of Three-in-one and Homousion,

To be lost in little walls and ricks of turf,
Dwindle down at peasant fires,
Huge ghosts in hungry fields
Wandering without memories.

No profit in it, or credit. Boors thrive
But I eat afield with the crows;
No goose gravy for Tom Euclid;
The master feasts on the hedgerows;

Yet, Pallas Athene, your true legionary
In the last earthworks, the lone garrison, still
Arrays himself in the delicate dactyls to
Decline you to the barbarian.

To the Boy

There's all this
Umbilical commotion, as if
One hung still by a living thread
To the mother or
A town almost forgotten

Come home
Back where meanings were
Tales told in the stigmata of
Souls near the Fall,
The harsh and beautiful;

So singing are
Streets that knew your rising, penny sweet-shops
And grocers' caves,
Those Norman walls on the edge of nothing,
The holy well and
The ruined abbey sitting on
The burnt-out rocket of a god.

So the Siren, pulling
At the tired old ravelling jersey, till
The wool is back in fleece on the old ewe,
Mother Ogre and womb of all.

Yet meet we must, though every Eden
Is a tree bleeding,
And the worse wounds are forgotten.

But my God there must have been
Some sweet bloom too
For a boy
Still to dangle in the bubble,

And, reborn and reborn as I may be,
After so many births

To wish him back, even if it be to see
Things as they are
And share this unbearable psyche
When we face all the big words together.

For we are near the taking off.

And it's time, time
To recover you who stood first
In this my skin
Tasting the early earth in
A world of wonders,

Matter itself shaping fair
The miracle, never this
Silent bombing round the clock.

So forgive me
If an old skeleton shambles home
Simply to remember you, to recollect;
Certainly there will be difficulties and no love lost,
For we're such strangers now.

Poems from Plays

The Young Gráinne

How can I define her?
A girl? A burst of sunrise in a room?
First breath of the apple tree? Or the first dawn
In the first garden pausing between two yews?
Or the virgin moment before strings are struck?

But those are the statements of innocence; and there is no
    innocence.
Who knows what lusts in the leaf and craves right-of-way
    through the bud?
Can sap be so simple that is old? Or innocent
The girl on her way to womanhood?
No, says the storyteller, blood is too old.

So hold the strings; they are too young for her.
She makes her own music standing up between
Two yew-trees, still as the dawn, a listener
Like Eve in that first garden, a design
In breasts and light between two sombre angels.

                    from *Diarmuid and Gráinne*

Gráinne On Slieve Echtge

I am on my knees in Echtge
Of the stones and birds. There are no trees.
The earth tugs me. Sky drowns my back.
Like grass I move slowly.

My breath in the ground; my knees
Bleed quietly by the hour.
Yet when I turn there is only the summer,
And every drop of my blood a flower.

                    from *Diarmuid and Gráinne*

Diarmuid in Flight from Fionn

Ah, the loving airy bay of Bran
The forerunner, gulper of light,
The water-walker whose weight is a ripple of wind,
Star of a dog who shines by night!

She comes not as an enemy,
This star at my heel. The bright eye, the drum sound
Of the mighty throat is a warning for me to hurry
Before they drag me numb to the dim ground.

                              from *Diarmuid and Gráinne*

The Sacred Berries

They are healing. They are renewal.
The first fuel of life. One berry –
Star like a wheel –
Will carry all time for a century.

Age peels like a skin from the old man.
The woman swarms like the queen bee.
There is laughter on the green, an oaken dance.
Gods break out in every tree.

                              from *Diarmuid and Gráinne*

The Widowhood of Gráinne

Mock her now; she does not care.
From the air about her falls this peacock stuff,
This wedding gown; O was it always here
But secretly, invisibly, on the hook
That now hangs naked as a lover's look?

How it settles about her. Did she really once
Disdain it, loving her boy, her very image
And prince of daylight; tearing this older man's
Lust from her back in rage
But to find it and all her wardrobe in a glitter at middle age?

194

The boy is dead, and so much lovely clay,
Arranging the attitudes of death, is a constellation;
But the marvellous head is a poor and bloody paste;
Who brought it to pass? The man? The woman? I must ask the
    question.

Was there always this death between the girl and boy?
Does death always lie by lover and lover?
And O, immense passivity of desire,
Was her bed, before the simple love was over,
Another night-life dreaming into the future?

I ask humbly: how much was innocence?
For only a little innocence could assuage
The drowsy god who nodded in the garden;
But when the tree gave tongue, did the words outrage?
No, for the woman spoke the language.

Now she unfolds herself in tall and jewelled glooms
Into her wish. And my heart stalls. Does a grave
Count, or a huddled boy, before this woman –
This slow magnificence in which I move
Dazzled, dazzled, as a boy in love?

from Diarmuid and Gráinne

Wet Lands

The dim country: what do we love in it
Who live in it?
The blank daylight? No. Nor in the daylight
The bog, its twilight.

No. And No. And yet a strong man
May find it kin
And never know it is his youth he loves
Till his youth leaves:

Never know that the woman on his hearth
Is only Earth
Good wife, good mother; and the farm he has –
The lover, never his.

The great unseasoned unseasonable bitch
In the last ditch
Always, and yet in a sudden day of sun
Almost to be won.

from The Poplar

Night and the Poplar

Good-night. Good-night, say
Good-night to the light of the day;
Noon with the burning face
And all earth in the grace
Of the tall bright air. The dark night
Is no old man's delight.

Who lives in the past? Why, none.
For who delights in the thing done?
And the thing to do is future tense
And the future is silence in every sense
When a man is old and given to things
That cannot follow his wanderings.

A rainy promise in the tree;
To the weather a farmer bows the knee
And lives in nerves that never stop
Living the life of every crop:
Let a tree speak of the weather, I
Hear and turn to the sky.

from The Poplar

Day of Rest

On Sunday the gates
Of quiet open and the slow sluices allow the tide
Of things to go its different gaits;
And earth shows her other side.

There might be Mass
In the air so peacefully does a country move
Inwards to the bell, slowly to pass
Up, like a smoke sucked surely from above.

Never are colours
More coloured; into them the young drive bicycles;
But the old are contented in their harbours
Of grass and the bright gusts that rise like angels.

from The Poplar

Water Diviner

O hazel twig, my gift
You, a fork of water in my hands,
More naked than a girl without her shift,
Find me a bright root under all lands

Find me the limb I lost
Long ago, the nymph of my garden, my cool
And marvellous one, my water-ghost
Hidden at the bottom of my soul.

from The Poplar

By the Water

Sally-trees, upthrust
Shadows of river-water, green as glass,
I, too, turned the dust
On its way upward through my waywardness
Into a person dressed
In his own tallness and his manliness.
But missed your comeliness.

Missed the delicate gait
That is content to stand upon one root,
Not hurrying to be late,
Not seeing outside itself the lovely brute
Who is always the mate
And always away, evasive, ever mute.
And I the fool who dances to her flute.

from The Poplar

Summer Delights the Scholar

(Vagans Loquitur)

Summer delights the scholar;
His knowledge is out of season;
He takes his task to the air;
He wanders by the river;

He reasons with rook and finch,
The thrush, the blackbird, sing for him;
His sober black turns green;
He chews a daisy chain;

Amply from his twig
He may admire the dawn;
See Lyra strung each night;
And praise the sweet musician;

Thus hedge-schooled he will find
A theme in what occurs,
The sylvan speech of God
Who sings the simple verse.

But back in candlelight again,
The pain of man will rear its head,
His vellums glow with fire and hail:
He hears the choirs sing for the dead.

from The Hags of Clough (final version)

Wayfarer

And where will you go this morning, sir?
And where will you sleep tonight?
If I lift up a shoe I've no warning, sir,
Where that shoe will alight.
I journey to God's good will, sir.

Jaunty your walk is, high is your head, sir;
Is it a lover you are?
Naught but a young fellow making his bed, sir,
And his future all in the air.
I journey to God's good will, sir.

Ah, the bed was made ere you were born, sir,
And the woman laid therein;
Go jaunt and go jingle and play on the horn, sir,
But all that will be has been.
Now journey to God's will, sir.

            from *The Hags of Clough* (early version)

The Seventh Son

O where are you going, my son?
Out on the world, my father dear.
Six sons I settled on it
And what will you do there?

O live upon them each in turn,
Yet ask no charity;
And each in turn when I rise to go
Will sigh regretfully.

For all must prosper where I stay,
None think I linger long
Who speaks words no one else can say
And turns them into song.

   from *The Hags of Clough* (early version)

199

The Last Drive

O many are dead, the gravedigger said,
And more are alive, alive O,
Who should lie here in the ring of my spade,
Dressed for the last, last drive, O.

For corpses they are though their heads in the air
Seem alive as a life is alive, O:
But the care that they carry, the dress that they wear
Is a shroud for the last last drive, O.

from *The Hags of Clough* (early version)

The Two Barons

Said the two bad Barons who loved one wife;
Fight, sir, or toss a coin.
Who wins will have the other man's life,
His castles, serfs and grain,
And the woman for his own.

Said the two Robber Barons to the lady who looked on;
We have fought to a standstill:
Wounds are more wonderful than woman
And pains great lauds that fill
The heart, the swelling chapel.

Said the two pale Barons lying on the ground:
Stop, sir, I give you all
But this my lovely sighing wound,
I am in love with my fall
And the sweet sounds of my soul.

from *The Hags of Clough* (early version)

Miserere

What shall I do? groans the penitent.
What shall I do? sighs his ghostly father.
If the trivial flesh is hell-bent,
Why all the fuss and bother?

I must repay, groans penitent.
What currency, my son? sighs father.
Your sin has gone and with it went
Most of the fuss and bother.

O, I am troubled, says penitent.
I too, I too, sighs father,
Seeing the wealth of time I've spent
On all this fuss and bother.

What if I die? says penitent.
What if you do? sings ghostly father.
You'll know the reason for devilment
And the use of fuss and bother.
  from *The Hags of Clough* (early version)

God's Sinners

Sinners all, the large and small,
Are God's children, sang the old Friar.
But only the believing man is tall
To gather lightning on the spire.
He is the lad will make his mark.
Amen, said the clerk.

There's neither luck nor leavings in
The reasonable sinner, sang the wandering Friar.
Give me the wild impulsive man
Who scatters all upon the fire.
God will inhabit the ruins at dark.
Amen, said the clerk.

There's Dick and Jim and Tom and Pat,
All careful men, said the silenced Friar,
Lean from labour and lack of fat,
They never know why God must hire
The sinful and idle to do his work.
Amen, said the dumb clerk.
  from *The Hags of Clough* (early version)

The Old Town

Castle Street, The Hill, The Mall,
The stone cell of the Tholsel, the Market Hall;
Trade is the adventure here,
Make tuppence of a penny and you're heir
To the hard-riding Norman who donned mail
Not for that chimera the Holy Grail
But for some hard-faced god who'd stride his church
On Sundays only, then clang out the porch
To bargain in the market and the square –
Make tuppence of a penny, you're his heir.
                            from *A Man in the Window*

Heart of Stone

What is it, what is it?
Tell me, Tholsel and Lane, tell me, Tower;
Black Church, what is the secret
Of the hard Norman heart,
The builder
Of this end where I start.

The old dark Burgher of a town
So rich a time and a time before me, you
Counting secret silver all alone,
False Smiler, admit me
For I, too,
Am a power and a mystery.

202

I take over your old stone
Mortared with moss, I ravish your decay,
And find I am all alone,
A conqueror no whit;
And you, with your day
Done, still master of the secret.

from *A Man in the Window*

Drowned at Sea

I have the usual
Premonitory shiver. The long green fathoms of my tongue
Would tell my tale of ebb and grow.
He died young.

Blue the arc-lamps of his eyes;
Slowly and with gravity he swells;
The sea and he indifferently a size;
Southward he falls, along his parallels;
I have the usual premonitory shiver,
Who died of too much water,
Who turns the globe in great bright water-wheels.

from *Outpost*

Starry Signs

I know the signs;
My boot rings on them; and what Orion keeps
Under his belt striding is no mystery
To a man walking when the world sleeps,
A star too between the lines.

Perseus with the writhe
Of that woman's face in his burning finger-bones,
Overhears the serpents inside
And the conversation of the terrible stones;
High he moves to catch his breath.

High on the hill
The helmet of Ares, the red ram and blue-eyed bull.
On the sea-limit the maiden and man's will;
Any wilful labouring man can pull
His starry weight by following his pole.

from Outpost

Dance of Opposites

Peace there is;
Appearances pieced together as one, concordance
Of world whose extremities
Deny one another but meet as one to dance.

Force to force
Allured, repelled, each dances, each opposite dances
Into its opposite, their centres
One yet never one, just keeping up appearances.

None dominant
Or earth would fall; the little steeples of the oats
Shed never a carilloned
Head or season, and the sea sink with the boats.

A dance is the face
Of the apple; the atomed and adamed tree is in step,
Buds pecking from boughs to base
And away; life in the rib and on the leap.

Peace there is, this
Dance that is all and everything, this war
Where small is great, where none collapses
Or must, where the general is most particular.

High wide and handsome
Earth turns, hoping for the best; O may
Our seasons still come
Round in their rhythm, with increase great and with decay.

from Outpost

Potato Rows

Potatoes, Kerr's Pinks, the royal
Champion, in rows, lines, little trees
Littering below the pole
Of light the penny-bright fruit of the fierce dark clays.

The horse bows
Into the collar, into the skies,
Into the gulls and the black crows.
A man sweats among the rows.

Oats, the name is Victory, has shot
Bolts and arrows, the target is the self
Unfolding; air takes the lot
And sky allows the limit; shoot and know yourself.

Man, man born
To the thorn and the terror, shoots his birth
Before him, O in what dizzy morn
Will he find it, he who sweats blood into earth?

from Outpost

Nightwalker

Pick my steps, Moon,
And shoe me. Heavy water my heart makes
That would sail true
To everything at once, for no sake but for all sakes.

So much noise and water
Sailing dog-lipped the capes of whales in white
Scud; shoe me, Moon,
And show bright the strands beyond where you fall quietly.

from Outpost

Whistling Buoy

The moaner on the shoal
Weedgrown rocks an obscene belly up and falls
Bullocking down again on the same hole,
And ever-sailing, going nowhere, wails.

At the tail of the race
Roars water sailing the white risk and never telling all
Tales to the rusted shell-encrusted face
That must rise weedy and must weedy fall.

from Outpost

Scent of Danger

What scent is that in the air?
A silence of hands and of hair
After her, too;
This is the body visible in the blue
Glance, the lovely unvirginal
Woman who knows nothing and knows all,
Divining me
With no love, with no pity.

Be silent before her, she
Still hears you and makes her mystery
Out of your own heart
And over before you wherever you start;
What scent is that in the air,
Invisible hands, invisible hair,
Never to succour me;
Ever my mystery. Ever aware of me.

from A Man in the Window

Love Song

If, O woman, you be mine,
Be always mine I pray;
Nor moonstray with the maidens
Who turn night into day.
Be mine, all mine, all time,
Till clocks and steeples nod;
O my grief, we do not walk as one
On Sunday before God.

from *A Man in the Window*

Tramp Poet

Bagman, beggarman going the road;
Bellman, balladman, town-crier;
How is one to know the poet
From his fellow, the common liar?

When had he his retinue?
O not since Asia was so young
The Gods came through the skin and through
The marvels on the poet's tongue.

Now like any soul in rags
And as big a fool as most,
He tramps the common road and begs;
Distracted by a mighty ghost.

from *The Bell for Mister Loss*

Midhir to Etáin

After winter I am the sun
Who wakens the cloudlike navy of the summer
And launches the tall flotilla of the swan
On every little water.

The lakes of Ireland are linked with wings,
Morning is royal where they settle
And evening dies the moated death of kings
Calmly in each small snow-whited castle.

Birds or towers, words that feather
Other words, all waters now
Plumed where skies are boating, clouds on a tether
Moored to a slowly curving prow.

This is me and my summer, lady.
I move through it into quiet things
All my reflections becalmed upon a heartbeat
So still, I am folded wings.

from *The Wooing of Etáin*

The Dying

Oh what a shambles, the dying repeat
To the dying. And is living only to die,
They ask of the moment for which they wait:
What shall we remember and what forget?
Best pray that the body have no afterwit
And that lover by lover lie
Obliviously, no alarm set
In the great stopped clock, Eternity.

from *The Seventh Step*

Translations and Versions
of Homeric Hymns

Homeric Hymns

The Stealing of Apollo's Castle

The maid Maia shook her head, here is
No cattle reiver, my lord Apollo, come
And see;

    And there was only
An empty cavern. Wait,
There was in the very plush centre
Tiny as a beam
Of sunlight in a pinhole, a small
Gold cradle that rocked itself.

My son, said the maid, a true
Lovechild to Zeus;
         And indeed there glowed
In the blues and saffrons of the quilts one
Small triumphant head.
         But three days old, said the maid.
And it seemed to the god
The air was filled with the lowing
Of cattle. Maiden, he said, my herds
Are nearby. Where?
         The thief was here,
Here he stood, so recently I can hear
Heifers chew the cud and drop dung –
         Maiden, said Apollo.

My Lord, said the bare truth in her, only Zeus
Comes here.

My cattle were or are in this cavern.

Lord, is Zeus a reiver?

                The god
Was staring at the infant in the cot.
Three days, he said, three days old and
Already a monster.
                Wake up, my newest brother,
And talk to me.
                Take your choice. Speak or
I throw you downstairs into Tartarus.
                                        I see
I do not discommode you, little thief.
                He shook the cradle noting
How the child rode it, all the rough and tumble.

So, child, you too are a power. In that case,
Let us speak as equals.

A great voice filled the cavern.
                My brother is
Too kind. How may we speak as man to man with this
Wet dribble down my chin?

Thunder in Heaven, said Apollo, you could be Heracles.

That thumper, said the babe. No, thank you. Could he
Hide from your all-seeing eye the two cowskins
I pegged outside to dry?

                My cows, the god whispered, the
Sacred ones.

                Who sacrificed when I was born? said the babe.
With Zeus, terrified of his old termagant, hiding
Us here in the wilderness.

                My child, my child, said Maia.

What other sacrifice would have relevance to
A major birth like mine?
                What other
Shake the heavens, give the place a new
Tilt?

Apollo hung over him in two wide wings.
You laugh, Babe, do you laugh at me?

No, said the little lad, should a child
Three days old, take on the big loud-spoken
Almighties? I haven't finished my
Disquisition with reference to your kine.

     The child sat up. He
Was quite luminous, already stretched
Far beyond the body.
              I thought, said he,
That heaven too should rejoice when I was born.
So I sacrificed your heifers to the Gods,
To the Twelve.

Apollo said, I see you want me to state
That we Olympians number only
Eleven.
       So the twelfth smoke
Arises for a three-day-old, a babe?

Ho, said the child, you shall have your cattle back
At once.

My cattle, Apollo answered, I have already.
Look into your mind, you will not find them there.

The child pondered. That's a trick, a right one
You'll have to teach me.

Some say, said Apollo,
With birch and ferrule. Well, I'm pleased
In one way to have met you, Number Twelve.
Goodbye.

You'll be back, said the babe.

The maiden Maia walked with the god, her face
Was full of wonder.
         What can I say, my Lord Apollo?

Behind, in the cave, the earth had begun
To dance, Apollo turned:
          A child making the music,
                              from
A shell, a simple shell
          (And that was the first string plucked)

I thought you'd be back, said the little one.
All desires pull.
                    And you want my shell. Here.

The music died, Apollo took the shell
Divining it,
          But could not find his way into a tune.

You'll have to teach me, said he.
Some say, said the babe,
With birch and ferrule. And one must be a god of course
Trees do not dance for common people.

O little cattle-robber, would you roast
Apollo in the sun?

          He laughed, the laughter going forth
In thunders that rapped the stone heads of hills
And rained in the valleys.

          Teach me, little brother, birch
Your sorry elder, but there's an art I must have.

You have it, said the Babe. Now
Quid pro quo, your royal herds for me.

Hey, said Apollo.

          The music stopped.
          So, said Apollo, you can stop me
As simply as that.

While the herds are yours, the gift and the shell
Are mine.

Ah, sighed the great god. I'll take the shell.
But tell me, wonder-babe, what will you do
With cattle, they're no toys, they're not exactly
Cradle playthings, what will you do with them?

Eat them, said the little lad. And grow up
To be like Daddy.
        This time however I reserve
The twelve best portions for myself, for Hermes,
He said modestly, the youngest and perhaps the fairest
Of the Gods.

Mercury and the Tortoise

The poor beast from its shell
He plucked forth;
        And he was only a boy, a babe,
The caul wet on him;
        Taking the item by
Its ridiculous throat, saying
'This is the way to make music';

        What remained in his hands
Was mother of pearl, a cool climate, a
Temperate sky
        Rounded as a mushroom, and almost
On the verge of song;
        (They were bubbling away unheard,
All those melodies, a well, I tell you
Music was on the way)

How did the holes appear, the strings
Stretched to the screws, that ride the bridge
Over the void where
The first note is born?

A boy, a babe in
A nimbus suddenly strung; and here he was
Taking the shell's own shape, the only true
Sounding board
World-wide at that, and then
By times a silly cockleshell.

The beastly meat
Still squirming, thumping out its own
Death throes.

How sweet.

Aphrodite on Ida

Things happen on mountains
If one is
Child or hero
And beautiful like Anchises;

Marble would ache for him, taking
The body golden
To its very heart, as he stood out
Harping. He was high up
In the morning
And she, the Goddess, on her
Way to fill ill-omened Troy.

Song or boy-man,
What caught her, after whom,
In the affluence of her going, creatures
Surpassed themselves coupling?

And what is man-flesh to the great spender,
To the cloud-burst?

They lay
On the coarse mountain twitch that turned
Into sweet cowlick under
Another shape.
Trefoil, that was it, and they
At once were three in one;

A miracle,
The seed of man inside the heavenly
Being who was suddenly
Sky and all.

Truly a miracle.

Rape of Persephone

And Zeus allowed it,
The Thunderer.
That the lord of Hell should know the touch of woman
In the groping shades:

Therefore this
Narcissus flower was born for her,
In the innocent grass
A most delicate snare;

It was alive, living;
A fountain of blossom;
And it grew just beyond her hand;
Tempting.

A servant could have plucked it:
She could have called,
But the buds seemed to jet
And be lost, only
To come again and be always there
In the presence:

It was the Presence caught her;
Hypnosis of
The whole person;
Lost, that was it, she was lost in
Her own flowering.

Then the mandate of the male
Reached her, earth
Was cloven at her feet, declivity
After declivity;

And everything, inside and out, was happening;
There was this man-head in her
Woman-body,

And vice-versa, she
Was the savage male she peacefully assuaged
In love's small handiwork.

Now as one they go
Gold chariot
Lighting something far beyond themselves.

Venus & Anchises: Afterthoughts

Tenderness?
               This rock-face of woman
Had none.
               'I have', it (she) spoke, 'fallen out of
My own grace. Now
I must endure the mockery of heaven.'

The divine body
Resumed its landscapes. Far below
He was listening to a quiverful of winter twigs.

Where was the lover gone,
The bountiful in whose bright year he
Had entered as a season?

'The Nymphs', she said, 'will rear
The Brat, think him blessed, pass him round
From tree to tree
For they can die,
                the thread-a-needle pine
The hungry thorn.'

The sated boy looked up.
                (So finite in
The spaces she assumed)

'In a little time they'll fetch him home to you;
You'll marvel then, you'll know
How near the heavens you were –

                as our boy
Towers out of burning Ilion, windy walls
And tall story.
                But tell how he was got,
Say how I groped for you and lay under
A mortal youth, while all my temples screamed

One after the other and my
Peacocks died –

And the shocked world shall not see
The bolt that falls on you.'

A Job of Journeywork

1.   *The Blind Old Man*

Maidens, it's now goodbye (be
Merciful, Apollo; and Artemis
Be kind, be kind). And if any should
Enquire which poet pleased you most
Of all who sang here, just say
A blind man who lives in Chios;
And I'll be told:

And in return tell of you
In city and island,
Your names shall sail, Maidens, while birds hang
Above the salt smacks or build
In the ears of princes, spreading like
The word of God.

(Spare me, Apollo, who am not for hire)

2.   *The Daughters of Keleus introduce the disguised
     Demeter into their Mother's household*

Metaneira, the mother, said yes, bring her; so
They leaped like arrows for the well
Where they'd left the strange lady;
And in bubbles of laughter they clustered
Round her (a tall Olympian,
Head covered, black-robed, heartbroken)
As she walked home with them:

And Metaneira
Waiting at a column, the high beams
Arching above the royal seat, with
Her new son fresh as a bud growing on
Her breast, saw her
Fill the door with the glory of heaven,
Lighting all
The shadows to the roof;

And in a panic of worship yielded her chair
Which, bless the carpenter, suddenly
Was flowering, its very timbers made of air.

To Dionysus

They fell on him,
Trembling from the black galley as it grounded,
A score of oars;
Pirates;
          surrounding him a youth in

His first brilliance, with
A king's ransom on his back
          (And they never questioned
          Why he dawdled in the spume) who smiled
Dreamily at them, remotely, offering no defence,
When they trussed him with their withy bands,
And remained unwrung.

They hove him down
On the dangerous thwart reserved for the God
(Oceanus whose gift he was to those half-finned fellows)
Where a void filled as if
A new ikon
Started up the old tremors,
          while they gloated, foolish men,
While they planned
Fortunes ahead.

It was the helmsman first saw the God,
The great gaze,
The space that gave him away
Behind the laughter

As the bonds lapsed and slithered down off
Limbs that suddenly
Were new dimensions,
          crying
Fools, fools, abase yourselves:

But they were snared already, caught
In a happening beyond belief: here was
          a deck sprouting
Green like Mother Earth;
          vines everywhere,
The budging mast was built of bloom, the sails
Were trellises of fruit,
They stood in
A deluge of the grape, smelling
Of winepress and vineyard, Spring and Fall
At once.

Meanwhile in the drunken air
The God's smile had broken.

The jape was over.

The great gaze that shared with them
Common sea and sky
Shattered

Like a mirror, and
Space gaped
In the pieces

Where one impious shipmaster grovelled,
Split into his elements,
Releasing one lion (retrograde) his tabu animal,
Vicious beast

Who bestrode the human bits, who
Consumed him utterly.
                    (Hail, Son of loveliest Semele)
And with his prey (videlicet
One impious shipmaster) vanishing

Into the God (perhaps)
                    (where else to go?)

Served some world purpose (perhaps)
Watched by the terrified crewmen,
                    overtaken in their turn;

Which event is
Chronicled since it tells
How dolphins came about;
                    (Sing Muse!)
Leaping whole, they say, a snouted array
Of fins and tails from
The salt laps of seamen, leaving

Behind nothing, except this fine tale and
Genus Delphinus, both new.
                    (Truly, Lord,
No one makes a song run true
As you who scotch the fakes.)

To Pan

There's a lynx skin
On the fellow's back. He sleeps raw
Has many terms of reference he denies,
Being in two
Places at once;

And not quite Olympian,
Indeed a very
Haphazard itinerant, shy of the main roads
You could pass him by where
He gossips in a wayside smoke.

But mark his face in
Your apple tree, that'll be dawn or dusk.
Only remember he has a dozen more
And can sit down with any simple girl
And turn her into a whore.

And how he dances full-bobbined on a well
With the Muses in the wild
Array he spreads around, and
The lovely girls are scattered, garments strewn
About him on the ground.

The entire lilting world will follow him.
Don't grudge your wife.
And let the budding girl foot the fallow;
Hoof and horns are good
In field and wood.

If the childless hear
The distant fluting clear and thin,
Wombs open. Here's the seed
Drops out of heaven on the ray of morning,
And the end of need.

Pan call him, Hermes' boy,
Capricorn has built him from the earliest
Model, from bits and pieces of the scrap-heaped gods,
A leftover, but the face
Was born of itself, is full of grace.

After Hesiod

The Muses' Gift

1.

And they that own
Helicon found me one day with my sheep,
Daughters of Zeus, saying:

If we want truth you'll tell it;
If a lie you'll think it truth and tell it:
It's as we will it;
We call the tune.

They gave me this rod
From the bay tree that never dies
And filled my mouth with the wonders of a god,

Bidding me sing of what never dies,
To tell all the past and the coming thing;
Always to call on them.

(But why, Tongue, go wandering
In an old wives' tale
Of tree or stone?)

2.

If they come to the cradle-head
Of the boy king,
His words later will be pure gold
And all will look to him;

He will interpret old things
Lay bare without earthly damage
A divine image:

225

Grey councillors will find their youth
In his every word of mouth;
Justice renew itself.

The singers and the harps belong to them
And Apollo.
(To Zeus the power-man, the king)
Lucky the prince if the cradle stirs
To such godmothers:

If he sing earth will know itself
In the resonance, the sick
Renew their names;

(Olympus is for all)

And the sundry insane forget
To be mad, treading
The new mountaintop.

After Pindar

Bellerophon

The miracle at last;
Pallas Athene
Flowing through his sleep, the ever-virgin,
A golden bridle in her hand.

What she bade him do he did,
Slew on the altar the bull she asked,
A great white beast full of seed;

Then from the earth's very centre he rose,
The god in him,
And made away to the well-side,
Where the famous stallion came to drink,
Untamed, uncatchable.

(From the Gorgon's head sprung,
Wings and all, fully fashioned, what mortal
Had a chance?)

Pirene's bubble was full of morning;
The Nine, unseen
Were seated for the spectacle,
A winged horse drifting from the zenith;

And suddenly in the air,
He was present, unstable, half evolved
From the puff of white vapour, from a cloud
On snow-white Olympus,

Yet all weighty flesh and bone
Checking his speed like
The singing swan falling towards the pool,
Winged legs up, taking the brunt,

Arriving where the Hero stood
Poseidon's son, Bellerophon, the gold
Bridle dangling;

What struggle in prospect
With that fierce mouth, already the mighty molars
Are bared, the unshod hooves
Erected; here was the
Tameless, the uncatchable, the immortal,

And the one regarded the other, then the bridle,
Gift of Athena, stirred
And of its own accord settled on the horse

Who bowed his head to it,
Took the yoke and drank at the clear spring
Where the Nine already
Had begun their song.

The Hyperboreans

Among them too are the Muses
For everywhere
To flute and string the young girls
Are dancing,
In their hair the gold leaves of the bay:

The dance whirls them away:
Age or disease, no toil,
Battle or ill-day's luck
Can touch them, they
Are holy, they
Will outlast time, exempted
From the anger of the Goddess
And all decay.

Here the hero came
With the head
That shocked a royal house, turning
King and all into stone:
It was long ago, if
Time means anything;
Long, long ago.

The Infant Heracles

Two serpents she sent,
Hera, Mother of the Gods,
And the child barely out of the womb

Lying haphazard like his twin brother
(Which was the immortal one?)
At his mother's bedside:

Doors opened to the great worms;
(There is no sanctuary from the gods)
Their shuffling rings in the midnight house
Scarcely a sibilance:

And nobody cried out in nightmare
When their fanged heads
Flickered at the cradle top;
No one gave the alarm;
The household slept;

But one child, a never-sleeper, crowed
And took from the air in growing and terrible hands
The sinister strikers;
By the napes he shook them
Till the wincing coils went slack,

And dropped them, like old rope, his twin
Bawling beside him, waking up
A commotion, which

Mounted Olympus, waking thrones,
And all the gods stared down while one looked up,
A new one

No longer indistinguishable, though
He shared the soothing dug with mortal flesh
And fell asleep.

After Theocritus

With the Gift of a Distaff

Good distaff, sprung first
From a whorl of Athena's thumb, Theocritus
Your poet is for Miletus, dingle of the Goddess, the
Love-woman of Kypris, and
Begs your company:

Have no fear of the uncertain sea;
Though Zeus distribute the uneven world
To every wind, beyond
The loom of the last island is our city and
Journey's end in
A friend's heart:

My comrade Nikias waits there for me;
And for you, Theugenis, his young wife who hails
From Syracuse, our own birthplace, the very
Navel of Sicily;
A simple girl full of grace.

O pleasing little ivory give yourself
To this lady, if only for a year,
And shepherds will double their flocks if only to keep pace
    with you,
And hill farmers
Look to the ram, for with you two as partners

Cloaks will dance off the buzzing loom
And precious undergarments hang
On the woman's line:
Distaff, I offer you no slattern's dwelling:
Here things live by the book

And Nikias holds forth, a master of medicine
Famous for his cures;
This is a notable house and I offer it

That my countrywoman, Theugenis, be renowned
For a distaff of such quality
That she must remember when she uses it
The poet, the giver,
Her visitor once, the singer of songs;

And Ionian housekeepers who see you spin
So large round such a tiny heart shall say,
'This, indeed, is a true gift
That multiplies itself in such
Huge increases day after day'.

Hylas

He was wielding
The forked twig when it pulled him
Down, mediterranean, where
Water sang.

It had a woman's voice, a girl's,
Two girls', three,
Many more; all about him
And no one to see;

Even when mouths were pressed on his,
Bodies were none;
He was the bubbling one;

He had divined them, now
Let them blow;
Let his breath forgive them

As they billowed, as they rose
And were made flesh
In earth above,

Nymphs of the moment
Of his death, who took their beauty
Out of his mouth

And danced, showing
Daffodil hair and roseleafed side
On the ripple

Where his name spread out in one
Broad vowel, somebody
Was calling him by name,

Hylas, Hylas,

But when he answered, knowing
From far off the hero whose sounds shook
His tender depths, his voice
Was water. Hylas

Had become a well.

After Callimachus

Erysichton

There was this youth who was I
And no way to dare
The Gods and bring them to the eye,
And make them aware.

So into her grave, axe high, I drove
The lovely body I was, the royal make,
And plucked her tree by tree;
The poplar first:

Be naked, I said, like me;
Match me in thigh, in eye, in high
Profile, and let one lose the other
In every form until we find the one;
What's love but the destruction of the world,
The unity of all in nothing?

She was there;
No lover, no mother, a woman,
That's all she was,

Composing my parts, a simple woman
Touching on all my points, enhancing
The little things I had forgotten;

My touch the more delicate, my eyes
A drift of the everyday most various world;
Stay this, I said. Let be.

But all of her was motion, she
Was passing, on the move and away, not
To be held,
The colours of seasons, the commons of the day,
Seen, wondered on, taken in
Most blindly indoors,
Where a woman should be
And a hearth.

That was the newest hunger,
To absorb her.

A life's work,
The appetite more and more. I ate
Up cities, my heart
Grabbed at states and realms, sprawled on
Continents,

While I lost sight and flesh and motion
And sit now
Bony hand out on the roadside.
Begging.

And nobody sees her;
All those passers-by with their small coins
And birds' eggs
Going up to the city

Walk right through the enormous body
That straddles the highway
That is Demeter my lady, my
Eternal hunger.

After Horace

Solvitur Acris Hiems

The first soft zephyr loosens the snowman's grip;
Ships roll down to the sea;
Cows leave the straw, the ploughman his ingle-nook;
The new pastures gaze through melting frost;

And Venus arrives in the sailing moon, with a wave
Of dancers, nymphs and Graces linked
To a naked beat, earth thrumming, while lame Vulcan spells
The blazing Cyclops at the furnaces.

And it's time to mingle in the happening, sport a twig
Of myrtle or a spring flower,
And remember Faunus with a lamb or a young kid,
Whichever he prefer:

For Death, dear Sestius, is always that much closer;
In hovel or tower a door
Will open of itself, there's no escaping, here
He stands with his phantoms waiting:

And no lucky throw will make you lord of a feast
Ever again; the dice are dead, the boy
Lycidas left to delight your enemy's eye
And all those girls at his feet.

Propertius to Ponticus

Who sings wars like Ponticus, echoing
The iron? Mars himself
Must hear and toe the line; your brothers
Say Troy's poet no better.
That's what they'll say, Ponticus,
If you're lucky.
Let me exalt you just in case.

For the Muses are choosy; being women
They blow about
And will hire out the horse to some Tom Thumb
Like me, a light fellow
Who could make do with a small
Palfrey or a spangled old pad
To trot round my ring; a palomino.

Any hack will do me
Who go round and round the same unceasing lady.
My God, what could I do
With a big prancing charger?
A lady in the air with me!
How could we do the trick without wings?

An old spavin, that's me;
A mania; with one burthen along
And the words that go with it;
The silly dizzy words of love. Pray God
You never have need of them.

If you have, what then? If
You go mad like me
Will the wit serve that launches
Cadres out where the map wilts,
Armour and catapults?
How would you deploy
What belongs to the chronicles of fallen cities

Where the city shifts,
Where towers are unreal and the soil flits at a word,
Where a long siege must sit down on nothing;
Where the objective
Is the small whorled gateway
Of a girl's ear;
And the tactics, my dear fellow, simply
A hatch of words like butterflies,
And a small sweet pipe?

Think of it, your bellowing warfronts bearing down
On a girl empty as a scrap of mirror
Who delicately as a tiny finch
Will titivate herself and sing on
Where bolts fall and legions
Grind to a halt,
Indifferent.

But come to it, the pain, too late
And you shall know
What a master I am in the little field
Where love wages the only
Campaigns worth talking about.
And even borrow from me

Leaving in your idle freightyard, huge
And rusting, the war's leftovers
For my sweet hatch.
Coming so late you'll have no words of your own;
And there is no market
Where one buys a vocabulary.

The circus gutters are rich in loose change;
Whores unpack themselves;
The broken gladiator weeps gold into a bottle.
A ponce is richer than you;
And you dare not stoop now
With all those dignities, panoplies and plumes,
Like this rake, your hailfellow,

Who, scratching at corners, coins
Himself as he goes,
Titters and pares his nails
And looks out at you
With the burnished face of Caesar.

Content that the youth of Rome
Continue to be born young,
Knowing they will haunt my tomb a while, crying
After Hic Iacet, we will never believe it,
That Propertius is gone;
Never till the last Roman virgin
Find an empty pillow in the bed
And cries out to the lamp, indeed, indeed,
Propertius is dead.

Who put the wick in oil
And shook night out of place
And brought out the lovelight
In every maiden face.

After The Archpoet
(Twelfth Century)

Confessio

Great anger shakes me.
I must allow it tongue
Hear me then, you men
Not yet hanged damned or wrung
I am made of light matter,
Light as a leaf, with the wings
Of a leaf and blown as one;
No longer my own master.

A wise man rides a thought,
Reins, unreins the steady horse;
But when I ride the saddle's
Just one more wing on my arse;
Any stir releases
The kites in me, O God
The air discourses no more
Than I in windy weather.

Thoughts mutiny, I stamp my poop,
Find no answer in the crew;
Thee sails take over up there
Like bird or cloud, blow through the blue;
No bonds, keys, gods
Can lock away my mind;
My thoughts deprave me, drive me
To seek my sinful kind.

The heavy weight of man
Has no room on my shoulders;
I seek the honeycomb, and must
Advance in roses;
Venus naked as a cloud
Or drenched in the coloured sea-wash moves
Me like a white shell shoreward,
Yet looms in the brightness leeward.

Before me, she. In the broad way
A glimpse where my youth goes;
She uses so many bodies
That turn to empty phrases;
Clichés! The flesh can't stand up
To all her meanings, her sudden poses;
She's sold me many a pup.
How do I still stand up?

And now again, smitten again; in love
With a young thing! Your pardon, Lord,
But here's the flower must heap my grave.
This girl's your earliest word,
You spoke it in the garden to a tree;
Here she is and I go down
Before your creation on one knee.
Here she is and I go down.

And ask nothing. O difficult to deny
This old boy raging in my skin.
A virgin! And I on one knee!
O Goddess, kick me on the shin,
Let Goatfoot take me over, Pan
Make tinwhistles of my thighbones;
Sing my shame among the fairies, but
My two knees are sinking down.

For this is Pavia. And you, friend,
You'll come, expecting to go chaste
Home, unburned, untarnished? What a hope,
Where every day's a waste
If Venus doesn't blossom in
A door or fill a street with
The marvellous body that shook the gate
Of Heaven – if we can believe the myth.

But try it, bring Hippolytus,
Chaste Hippolytus, to Pavia;
Give him the reins – and see him eat the bridle;
Look for him *sequente die*,
In the first light, or the second light. No
Hippolytus, bird flown.

240

For of all the towers in Pavia there's none
Was raised to chastity, not one.

You raise, too, the matter of my gambling.
Right, I admit. The dawn and I
Have shared a naked bench together
With the first snail horning at the sky
Often, Boy, and my only coat in pawn;
And yet with the frost at full bite have found
Such profundity, forgotten it
In the heat of verse, the beaten anvil's sound.

My drinking too? Don't leave that out.
Impeach me – liquidly.
I'm given to it, yield without fight.
My measures don't lack quantity.
What if a second head comes over mine,
The drunken mask of Faunus, he's a friend;
When angels sing my requiem,
He'll be there, Boy, puking to the end.

Meum est propositum – I mean
In the vernacular, let me die drunk
Struck by Jove's thunderstone the bottle,
After some words with that same lordly skunk.
If you're given to angels, here you'll see them
Heartbroken, their feathers round me,
Singing, God is good to this
Tavern fellow, *huic potatori.*

A lamp shines in the cup.
It animates the ghost
That gives, on second thoughts, a fellow wings
To meet (on second thoughts) the holy host.
Sweet is the glass I pour
In my sacred corner with a whore,
A halo on it, wings, no mitre.
(The bishop's stuff but feeds a goitre.)

I know that poets full of grace
Should leave the tavern to the fool;
I know that poets full of grace
Should leave the forum to the fool;

I know that poets full of grace
Should pare the quill, prepare the ink,
Write epics with a pious face;
And never never die of drink.

Dear Friend, it's not that way at all.
Good verse never wore
Its halo with a saintly tilt.
When did Apollo love a bore?
Is a hungry belly free to think?
Where does a rhyme start? On whose feet
Does Bacchus stagger out to drink?
Don't the heavens sup when a poet stands treat?

So fast you for me, since I
Must spread my rhymes from a full bag.
If guts are hollow wind accrues,
Fast you for me;
With your great gift for nothing hunger goes,
Therefore fast, boy;
And let me fatten against the rutting time
When poems mill round me like wild does.

And that's my case, my head
Plain on the platter. All can see now
The errors of my soulcase.
I do accuse myself.
But add to this; I'm judge and jury, Lord,
And in all dignity look down my throne
On the drunken whoremongering sinner, Me,
And passing sentence say, Live on, Live on!

After Gérard de Nerval

Vers Dorés

One for Helen

Man the Thinker! You think yourself the sole
Thinker in a world where all things think to be?
The powers you are have given you liberty,
But you leave Nature out that makes the whole:

Regard the beast and how a spirit moves him;
Each flower hatched by the humble earth's a soul;
In metals repose Love's mystery and fall:
All's sensible, cries Pythagoras. We share a dream.

The eye looks out on you from a blind wall;
In matter the Holy Word is working still –
Careful! it's delicate and must serve no ill.

Often the god inhabits the dark inside,
Under night's lids the great light-bearing ball,
Under the skins of stones the living tide.

After Baudelaire

The Cat

My time was then, before Earth tamed volcanoes
To fold their petals quietly as a rose,
When from her loves Nature had who knows
What strange children in mighty ebbs and flows.

I could have been a cat, voluptuously
Curious on the knees of a huge young queen
While she flowered in large sweet tremors under me,
Wooed but wondering, lost, and longingly obscene.

To trouble her look with a male and secret stare,
Green as glass, and then, O love, to wander
The great valleys of her loosening knees

Or sometimes in summer evenings when she rests
Stretched out like a countryside, to take my ease
Like a sleepy mountain village on her breasts.

Parfum Exotique

Your body this humid afternoon is another
Climate, your breast a tropic I take over,
Geography a sultry odour, aromas of you where
I lie headlong on a new-found equator;

An island listing to the Trades drops fruit
Down the tilted South; big mincing bucks
Laze on the skyline and your blood-sisters flit
By, outstaring me with insolent good looks;

Here are the regions native to your flesh,
A drugged seahaven, ships at the wall
With cockbilled yards, broken from seas too tall;

And the green tamarinds, the odour of – and the mess
Mix in the salt world drifting off your skin
With the sailaway chanties of the deepwater men.

A Bird for Nancy
(L'Albatros)

Often for devilment old salts might snare
An albatross, the big white ocean bird
Following after, supreme voyager,
Dangling his indolent carriage over the surge.

Scarcely is the great winged creature down
Than the grace goes; a flapping huddled thing
On wooden pinions oaring itself along,
The flight, the royal repose, the tilt all gone.

This feathered traveller how maladroit afoot,
Fellow of the air, so lately beautiful;
One thrusts a smoking claypipe down his throat;
And one apes the flight of the poor earthbound fool.

And that's the image, Poet; a prince in the air
You laugh down the gale at the archer and his bow;
But on earth a butt for every hoot and stare,
Wings useless, and no real place to go.

Two Mallarmé Things for Sue

The flesh is sad. I have read all the books.
It's a jacked-up world. Even the birds sling their hooks.
And I could do with a trip to unknown skies;

There's nothing. Even the gardens of your eyes,
No lie, hold my glance no more. The damp's
In everything, even the lamp's
Empty room on the white page. (The poem's
Dead against me, help me God.) Home's
No longer where the doll is dishing out
The baby's bowl of stout.
                                    I'll leave, by Christ
The next boat's mine. I'll see I keep the tryst.

Bored to the tits, sick of the same old guff,
I'd love a whole dockland to wave me off.
The winds are welcome to my perch;
I know the earth by my legs' sea-lurch;
It's shipwrecked, Mates, and heaved along
By nothing more than a sailor's song.

2.

Primitive spring lays winter in sad waste,
My most civil winter, season of lucid things;
And in my distressed man the new tide brings
The impotence of a world gone double-faced.

The white corpuscles roar round my head;
I've haloes of iron on my unlaurelled brow;
I'm the sad joker with the unbent bow
In the broad champaigns where the dews can raise the dead.

The huge mad dancing dews, and me with a dream
Following after, falling unnerved to the trees,
Given to the earth and the odours, going along with the stream.

I bite holes where lilacs must sink roots,
And know how I beam when my hedges blow to the breeze
And birds in a thousand blossoms clamour on the shoots.

After Rimbaud

Ma Bohême

So I tramped the roads, my hands through my torn pockets
My old coat just a ghost about to vanish;
I was your tramp, Muse, but rich, with worlds to lavish,
La, la, the marvels we dream of, we mad poets!

I rhymed with my buttocks falling out like moons
Through holes in my trousers, uncaring, my head in the air;
I took a room each night in the Great Bear;
Stars over my distant hair had the soft swish of gowns.

And I listened, excited with dew as with strong wine,
At my ease in a ditch, a mood, a creature of starshine
In the good September twilights, a man apart,

And rhyming, rhyming, while all the darks took root,
I tucked one leg like a lyre about my heart
And strummed the elastic of my broken boot.

O Saisons, O Châteaux

O Seasons, O Châteaux,
What angel is there will not fall low?

O Seasons, O Châteaux,

I have made a magic study
Of the good thing that eludes nobody;

Sing it every time you hear
The gallic cock its chanticleer;

Me, I have no will at all,
It's taken me over body and soul,

A spell usurping whatever I be
Blows all abroad, dispersing me,

So that to understand a word
You flee and follow like a bird.

Seasons O, and O Châteaux.

After the Medieval Irish

Columcille the Scribe

My hand is weary with writing;
The light quill twitters in my fingers;
Yet here, still, my slender-mouthed pen
Pours a draught for me of dark-blue ink.

My brown hand – O blessed it is indeed
With the stream of God's wisdom pouring from it! –
Squirting the brightness of many inks,
Moves happily till leaf after leaf is lit.

Ah, my little pen, it moves on
Across the plain of books in holy words,
And without ceasing makes, though I am tired,
Cyphers that suddenly take wings like birds.

After the Irish of Raftery

Mary Hynes

That Sunday, on my oath, the rain was a heavy overcoat
On a poor poet, and when the rain began
In fleeces of water to buckleap like a goat
I was only a walking penance reaching Kiltartan;
And there, so suddenly that my cold spine
Broke out on the arch of my back in a rainbow,
This woman surged out of the day with so much sunlight
I was nailed there like a scarecrow,

But I found my tongue and the breath to balance it
And I said: 'If I bow to you with this lump of rain
I'll fall on my collarbone, but look, I'll chance it,
And after falling, bow again.'
She laughed, ah, she was gracious, and softly she said to me,
'For all your lovely talking I go marketing with an ass,
I'm no hill-queen, alas, or Ireland, that grass widow,
So hurry on, sweet Raftery, or you'll keep me late for Mass!'

The parish priest has blamed me for missing second Mass
And the bell talking on the rope of the steeple,
But the tonsure of the poet is the bright crash
Of love that blinds the irons on his belfry,
Were I making an Aisling I'd tell the tale of her hair,
But now I've grown careful of my listeners
So I pass over one long day and the rainy air
Where we sheltered in whispers.

When we left the dark evening at last outside her door,
She lighted a lamp though a gaming company
Could have sighted each trump by the light of her un-shawled
    poll,
And indeed she welcomed me
With a big quart bottle and I mooned there over glasses
Till she took that bird, the phoenix, from the spit;
And 'Raftery', she says, 'a feast is no bad dowry,
Sit down now and taste it!'

If I praised Ballylea before it was only for the mountains
Where I broke horses and ran wild,
And not for its seven crooked smoky houses
Where seven crones are tied
All day to the listening top of a half door,
And nothing to be heard or seen
But the drowsy dropping of water
And a gander on the green.

But, Boys! I was blind as a kitten till last Sunday.
This town is earth's navel!
Seven palaces are thatched there of a Monday,
And O the seven queens whose pale
Proud faces with their seven glimmering sisters,
The Pleiads, light the evening where they stroll,
And one can find the well by their wet footprints,
And make one's soul;

For Mary Hynes, rising, gathers up there
Her ripening body from all the love stories;
And, rinsing herself at morning, shakes her hair
And stirs the old gay books in libraries;
And what shall I do with sweet Boccaccio?
And shall I send Ovid back to school again
With a new headline for his copybook,
And a new pain?

Like a nun she will play you a sweet tune on a spinet,
And from such grasshopper music leap
Like Herod's hussy who fancied a saint's head
For grace after meat;
Yet she'll peg out a line of clothes on a windy morning
And by noonday put them ironed in the chest,
And you'll swear by her white fingers she does nothing
But take her fill of rest.

And I'll wager now that my song is ended,
Loughrea, that old dead city where the weavers
Have pined at the mouldering looms since Helen broke the thread,
Will be piled again with silver fleeces:
O the new coats and big horses! The raving and the ribbons!
And Ballylea in hubbub and uproar!
And may Raftery be dead if he's not there to ruffle it
On his own mare, Shank's mare, that never needs a spur!

But ah, sweet Light, though your face coins
My heart's very metals, isn't it folly without pardon
For Raftery to sing so that men, east and west, come
Spying on your vegetable garden?
We could be so quiet in your chimney corner –
Yet how could a poet hold you any more than the sun,
Burning in the big bright hazy heart of harvest,
Could be tied in a henrun?

Bless your poet and let him go!
He'll never stack a haggard with his breath:
His thatch of words will not keep rain or snow
Out of the house, or keep back death.
But Raftery, rising, curses as he sees you
Stir the fire and wash delph,
That he was bred a poet whose selfish trade it is
To keep no beauty to himself.

Raftery's Dialogue with the Whiskey

RAFTERY

If you shortened many a road and put a halo
On every thought that was growing in my head
Have I not been to you as the brown nut to the hazel?
Your fruit, O my comrade?
And in many a lonely bed have I not praised you
With sleepy words no virgin ever heard?
And after all this, O the spite of it, here in Kilcreest
You topple a tallow candle and burn my beard.

Troy in its tall sticks never burned with a blaze
As bright as Raftery's hairs when that evil spark
Leaped on his skull and from that holy rooftree
Pitchforked his spluttering thatch;
Shame on you! not even Mercury who rose
Out of the cradle to fall on evil ways,
Stealing cattle, would hobble my wits and roast them
Hide and hair like that in the fire of my face.

O I was the sight then and the great commotion;
Wells running dry and poor people peeling their legs
With barrels and pails, and the fish flying down to the ocean;
And look at me now! a mere plaster of white of eggs!
Look at me! a bonfire to folly! but no man
Was ever saint till he was a sinner first;
And I'll break with you now though it cost me the mannerly
　　company
Of the gay talkers who follow a thirst.

So I dismiss you. Here! Take your mouth from my mouth!

I have weighed you, O creature of air, and the weighman cries,
'Here's nothing will balance a holding of land in the south
Beef on the hoof there and grass climbing up to the skies;
What's whiskey to hanging bacon?
To a glittering hearth and blue delphware?
Will it put a Sunday coat on any man,
I ask you, or leave him to walk bare?'

Ah, sweet whisperer, my dear wanton, I
Have followed you, shawled in your warmth, since I left the
　　breast
Been toady for you and pet bully
And a woeful heartscald to the parish priest;
And look! If I took the mint by storm and spent it,
Heaping on you in one wild night the dazzle of a king's whore,
And returned next morning with no money for a curer,
Your Publican would throw me out of the door.

THE WHISKEY

You blow hot and cold, grumbling,
The privilege of the woman and the poet.
Now let me advise you, Man of fancy stomach,
Carry a can and milk a nanny goat!
Drink milk! for I am not for you – as I am not indeed
For your brother the miser; but, ah, when the miser's heir
Grows into manhood and squanders I'll walk through the
　　company
And call that man my dear.

254

I grow too heady now for your grey blood;
And you do little good to my reputation
With your knock-knees and tremulous jowls – for God's sake
Pay the tailor to press your pelt and tuck it in!
What can I be to you now but a young wife to an old man?
Leave me to the roarers in the great universities,
The masters of Latin with the big ferrules
Who know what use strong whiskey is!

Hush, now! I'll speak or burst. You have no pith,
And I pity the botch of a carpenter who planed you down.
You are maudlin at table ere the company is lit,
And among clowns, the heaviest clown.
I have given you pleasure, yet you round on me like a lackey
Who will swear he was overworked and underpaid;
And tomorrow, O most grievous insult of all, you'll repent of me
That the priest may help you into a holy grave.

RAFTERY

Ah, that tongue was sharpened in many a bad house
Where candles are hooded on the black quays of the world;
Many is the sailor it stripped to the bleak hose
And the Light Dragoon with his feather furled;
I hear it now and I pray that a great bishop
Will rise with a golden crook and rout you out of the land
Yourself and the rising family of your sins,
As Patrick drove the worms out of Ireland.

You're an illness, a cancer, a canker, a poison,
Galloping consumption, broken breath,
Indiaman's liver, thin diseases of the person,
Cholera Morbus and the yellow death;
You're the two sour women who wait here by my mattress
With Christian charity and broken hen-eggs
To mess my only features, but if I live to denounce you
I'll empty every tavern when I get upon my legs.

THE WHISKEY

If hard words broke bones every sad rascal
With a bleached tongue who turns on me of a morning
Would have done for me long ago, yet I rise again like the pasch
Quietly, brightly, in their minds and they return.

RAFTERY

Who returns but the shiftless drifters, the moon's men?
Stray calves who'd suck at any udder?
Waifs, bagmen, beggars, and an odd fool of a lord
Crazy enough not to know better?

THE WHISKEY

Men of merriment, the wide girthed men
Whose eyes pen cattle, and slender men who hold
The curves of a filly together with one finger
While the other strips an heiress of her gold;
Equal those, O Fiddler, men of the great gay world
Who can dance a stately figure or bow prettily to a queen
And keep fine manners though the blood be rearing
Like a red stallion on the fair green.

RAFTERY

Blackguards, rakes, who rise up from cards
Only when the sun is trumped there on the table
Like the red ace of hearts, take them, the gamblers
Who wouldn't pay their debts were they able;
Dicers, procurers, who'll give you an I.O.U.
On the honour or dishonour of a wife or daughter,
Take them, the lot of them, hog, devil, or dog,
And drown them in a bucket of bog water.

THE WHISKEY

Poets and musicians –

and absentee landlords,
Militiamen on hayfeet-strawfeet who burn
Brightly as red lamps in a lanewife's back parlour,
Taking, as always, the wrong turn;
I leave you to them and to the landlord's agent
Who shivers beside you day-in day-out
Walled in by the hostile murmurs of the rainy grasslands
In an old windy house.

THE WHISKEY

For a homespun poet whose pride I nursed
When doors were shut on him and dogs barked at his heels,
Your gratitude is such I'll swear a cutpurse was your father.
And your mother the lady who tied eels.
Desert me, indeed? You windy bag of old words,
You wan wizened weasel with one worn tooth!
If I whistled tomorrow you'd hobble to me on your sores;
And that's the truth.

RAFTERY

Whistle then!

THE WHISKEY

I'll whistle when
I'm in the mood

RAFTERY

Whistle! Whistle!

THE WHISKEY

Maybe when you've money and can spend,
When you're a farmer slaughtering the poor thistle,
Stoning crows or coaxing cows,
Counting your corn grain by grain,
With thirteen bonhams to every one of your sows,
And you carrying a big purse at the fair.

RAFTERY

Good-bye for ever then!

THE WHISKEY

Good-bye Raftery.

RAFTERY

I'll never be a farmer.

THE WHISKEY

And where is the need?
Poetry and whiskey have lived always on the country.
Why wouldn't they indeed?

RAFTERY

You're right. Why shouldn't I tax the heavy farmer?
I give him wit. And you? You give him – what?

THE WHISKEY

No matter. We are two necessary luxuries.

RAFTERY

Listen! I'll drink to that.

Ballads

For Ireland I'd Not Tell Her Name

Air: Irish Music & Song (Joyce, page 23)

"'S in Éirinn ní inneosainn cí hí"

In the dews of last night and I moving
Through a holding of land not my own,
A maiden I met, my undoing,
My illness, my wild wishing-stone;
And my sleep in a wave that has washed
Up a moon on the strand, and I stare
All night on a water-bright face;
Yet for Ireland I'd not tell her name.

If she'd only allow me a whisper
It's a sweet and mad music she'd know;
The heart is the fiddler who fiddled
For the lady who laid Troy town low:
O Maiden, the story is love,
The burning of lamps and the blame,
With a thunderbolt waiting above;
Yet for Ireland I'd not tell her name.

One mile from my mearings she lives,
And the moon is a mile nearer me;
Still the man who goes all round his beads
Will touch on the last Mystery:
Oh, I fear her, the way that she strolls
And the body that rumours her fame:
Yet I linger long whiles by her walls;
And for Ireland I'd not tell her name.

O Maiden, O Maiden, I'll plough
And I'll manage your place if you will
With grass growing green on the mountain
And a walk of stone steps to the wall:
But O I am stripped like a pole,
My blood is red rust in each vein;
I nod and I rock like a fool;
Yet for Ireland I'd not tell your name.

The Hen and the Cock

Air: Amhráin Muighe Sheola No. 0

A hen and a cock they did set off together,
walking all Ireland to see what they saw;
arriving in Galway in very low feather,
for strollers they're taken and locked up by law.

With William O'Heelan 'tis where they were grazing,
eating his berries without any pay;
the sheriff in tunic and boots came a-grazing,
and in the black hole he did lock them away.

Oh great was that cock above all in this country;
spurs he did wear of white silver from Spain,
a straw hat and gloves and a whip were his whimsy
the day he'd decide for to strut to a fair.

It's down there at Millbrook you'd hear them to praise him,
women who're drinking the blue buttermilk;
my soul for that fellow, they say he's from Asia,
he treads our wild ways though his spurs walked on silk.

Oh golden that cock above all in this nation;
worlds he'd awaken and crow down a barn;
no jail it would hold him or be his damnation;
but hungry old women they brought him to harm.

'Twas down at Slieve Bawn that he chanced to be strolling,
noble the hen-bird that tended his pranks;
those monsters they coaxed him, they petted and stroked him,
then led home the King with a rope to his shanks.

Oh why did they need him and mutton a-begging,
beef at the butcher's and hens by the score?
They pulled off his feathers, his head got a wigging,
and still, they do say, that he sang by the door.

My curse on the day. Oh the buttermilk ladies,
beggars and naygurs who throng the back door;
they tore him to pieces for salt for their praties,
and danced round the nation to show his back bone.

The hen she did lay us a hundred eggs daily,
queen of quadrilles when she'd dance on one leg,
is moping and drooping so haggard and pale she
will never no more sit her down on an egg.

Oh why did you ate him? What good luck can follow?
Gold was my cock's head, the stars made his tail;
the King of Creation with never his fellow
and since he was murdered the country does fail.

The clergy will blame you, O women of Mayo;
walk over the nation and see all the harm;
each hen on her perch, never saying her prayers,
but wings hanging down, her head under her arm.

Oh rich was that cock and what stomach can hold him
headstone or spade will not lay him away;
Oh furious women! A little red hen says,
you'll meet a great cock on the highroad some day.

Buachaillín Bán

The buachaillín bawn he
Is going from me,
His spade he sold and his boots are on
He'll tramp his passage
Down to the sea-side
And find a ship there some early dawn;
Soon he'll be sailing
The round white day-ring
To Amerikay, oh my buachailleen bawn.

The buachaillin bawn
The tall, the fair one,
His spade he sold and his boots are on,
In yellow leather
His hat a-feather
He's all for travelling to Boston Town
Farewell, my darling,
Away I'm faring
A coach and coachman you will see soon

With four white horses
To make their courses
Before your door, with the buachailleen bawn.

The buachaillín bawn,
Fair one, O tall one
It's he went faring with three crowns or more;
A maiden met he,
Tall jack-a-dandy
　　　　　fared
It's he went forth with no crowns at all
A maiden met he
Tall jack-a-dandy
A farmer's daughter was his downfall.
Oh you must marry
With her you tarry
And leave the other you prate upon;
I've gold and riches
And hanging flitches
And all for you, Oh, my buachailleen bawn.

The buachailleen bawn
Has risen by dawn
He ploughs, he's mowing, all things to right
His only course is
Behind two horses
And naught to spend of a market night;
His breeches yellow
Would fit a fellow
Three times his size did he put them on;
Oh, high he married
The day he tarried
But low he lives now the buachailleen bawn.

Afterword

Padraic Fallon was born in Athenry, Co. Galway, on 3 January 1905. His father was a fairly well-to-do cattle-and-sheep dealer or "jobber", and the family also owned a hotel and butchering business in the town. The poet's early life was typical in some ways of that section of the new Ireland which was moving from the land to the towns and cities, forming a new bourgeoisie. After schooling at a boarding college in Ballinasloe and at the Cistercian college in Roscrea – a rather spartan regime which left its mark – he moved to Dublin, and became, at the age of eighteen, a civil servant in the Customs and Excise, based in Gandon's 18th-century Custom House on the quays.

His move to Dublin coincided with the stablisation of the Irish Free State after the Civil War and a decade of violence generally, beginning with the 1913 gun-runniing which had led in turn to the 1916 Rising and the ensuing dour guerrilla struggle of the War of Independence. His family was mainly Home Rule, and he himself was a schoolboy during the actual fighting, but he was stirred deeply by the heady feeling of national rebirth, political and cultural. However, he was always clearheaded about the War of Independence and its real roots and impetus; in essence he saw it as a land war and a class struggle, fought primarily against the Anglo-Irish ruling and landowning class rather than against England.

He seems to have written verse from his early teens, and he had his first intuition of the power of poetry when hearing a Latin teacher use the (rather hackneyed) phrase "lofty ships" while translating a passage from Virgil. His first literary sponsor in Dublin was that very remarkable man "AE" (George William Russell), poet, pamphleteer, social prophet, religious mystic, newspaper editor, agricultural reformer, and of course literary godfather to more than half intellectual Dublin. Russell encouraged him to find himself, invited him to "at homes" in his house where he met other writers, and was instrumental in getting his first poems published. More than that, his spacious, benign and magnetically sympathetic personality exercised a lifelong influence on Fallon, and it was from Russell that he derived much of his preoccupation with Oriental religion and thought.

In 1930 he married Dorothea ("Don") Maher, the daughter of a

265

Dublin builder, and moved north to a posting in Cootehill, Co. Cavan, where his two eldest sons were born (I am the second). In 1936 he moved back to another post in the Custom House in Dublin, living at this time in Sutton, just north of the capital. He had met and become friendly with "Seumas O'Sullivan" (James Sullivan Starkey), editor of the *Dublin Magazine*, and his wife, the gifted painter Estella Solomons; poems, short stories, articles and reviews by him appeared regularly in the magazine until it folded with Sullivan's death in 1958.

In 1939 he left Dublin again to take up a post in Wexford, on the south-east coast, and remained there until 1963 when he moved back to Dublin for the last time. He did not readjust to it and to literary life there – perhaps he was aware of becoming an unfashionable figure, or perhaps he had simply lost interest in the Irish literary milieu as such – and in 1967 went to live in Cornwall, a few miles from Penzance (his artist son Conor had already settled there and a close friend, the painter Tony O'Malley, lived not far off in St Ives). A combination of nostalgia for Ireland with certain other factors drove him back in 1971 to settle in Kinsale, Co. Cork, which had a flavour of the small-port life that had always appealed to him. But his intuition, or superstition, that he would die in Ireland proved false. A lung operation had left him weakened in health, and while visiting his fifth son, Ivan, in Kent he contracted an infection which developed into pneumonia and led to his death in hospital at Aylesford, Kent, on 8 October 1974, a few months short of his 70th birthday. His body was taken back to Kinsale and he is buried within sight of the Atlantic.

On the face of it, Padraic Fallon led an uneventful life and even a provincial one (he only visited the Continent once, and that was near the end of his life, when he made a trip to France). This was not entirely untypical of his generation of Irish writers, in spite of Beckett's voluntary exile in France, Francis Stuart's wartime years in Germany, the international exploits of Liam O'Flaherty, the American career of Frank O'Connor and others. The War years, the relative poverty of the 1930s and the austerity of the 1950s, kept many writers and painters chained to their desks, their jobs, their families, their easels, with nothing more cosmopolitan by way of contrast than an occasional visit to London, or at most to Paris.

However, this begins to sound all too like the conventional idea of the Irish writer-who-never-got-away. Padraic Fallon certainly did not regard himself as a victim of circumstance; he was not of the stuff emigré writers are made of, and his deepest roots and his material lay partly in the Irish countryside and small towns, partly in the timeless world of myth and philosophy. He was as much at home with farmers, fishermen and old sailormen as he was with fellow-writers, as happy playing poker with the Wexford bourgeoisie as he was in the company of the various cosmopolitan Americans with whom he mixed in Dublin in the postwar years.

In spite of his admiration for French culture, which was typical of his generation, I cannot imagine him settling into emigré life in Paris as some of his friends did; and while America would certainly have stimulated him, its scale and impersonality would probably have repelled him in the short rather than in the long run. Wide-ranging in his reading and interests, he was home-loving and almost insular in his life-style – even his voluntary exile to Cornwall did not last very long.

Padraic Fallon is a deeply original poet without being in any sense a revolutionary. His writing career spanned half a century and began in the late glow of the Celtic Twilight, whose conventions still dominated the milieu in which he moved and wrote. It is notable that while AE was to a large extent his first intellectual mentor and master, there is virtually no influence from AE's poetry (which, in later life, he used to describe as a "vague blue landscape"). The broad shadow of Yeats hung right athwart his generation of Irish poets, though Yeats with his hieratic airs and increasing social snobbery kept a distance between himself and the young writers of the new, *arriviste* Ireland such as Fallon and Austin Clarke.

Yeats marks approximately the boundary of that epoch in which Irish and English literature were still close enough to be barely divisible from one another; Padraic Fallon is one of the earliest – and to my mind, the most important – Irish poets whose sensibility is essentially un-English. This does not imply hostility to English culture; on the contrary, he was soaked in the English poets, from the Elizabethans and Metaphysicals down to the Romantics and beyond. Fallon had every notable English and American poet of the century on his shelves, and even in his sixties he was capable of being excited by his discovery of Sylvia Plath, but he has no more in common with Wallace Stevens or Hart Crane than he has with Betjeman or Philip Larkin. (Neither, to be sure, has he much in common with his fellow-Celts, Hugh MacDiarmid and Dylan Thomas.)

Partly a personal factor, partly an Irish Revival inheritance, is the folk element which plays so important a part in his work. On the face of it, this seems an unlikely co-habitant with the often esoteric philosophy, the wide-flung mythological references, and the genial but sometimes cerebral irony which are all characteristics of his mature style. Yet folk influences have been part of Irish literature, both in Gaelic and in English, for centuries, and one of the source-books of the whole Literary Revival was Douglas Hyde's book of translations, *The Love Songs of Connaught* – which can be said to have had the same importance in this context as the Arnim-Brentano collection *Des Knaben Wunderhorn* had in the development of German Romantic poetry. In this respect, Irish literature is closer to German and Spanish literature than it is to English or French. In Spain, for instance, it was possible for Lorca to combine Andalusian folk imagery and folk metres with the most "advanced" poetic idiom of his own time, *Cante Hondo* with Surrealism; and I am told that even in Brecht's work – which one would have thought to be essentially an art born of urban, industrial civilisation – the folk element remains strong.

Yeats, of course, had propagandised on behalf of Irish folk culture, but his use of it was often stilted, self-conscious and "literary". With the exception of a handful of lyrics (mostly early) and the play *The Countess Kathleen*, he does not convince us that it is his world. He remained the Irish Protestant burgher in his frock coat, the visitor to the Big House hunting for copy among the local peasantry. But Padraic Fallon was a countryman by background and ancestry who grew up in a world where the tramp-poet Raftery was still a fairly recent memory, and Gaelic folk-song was a living tradition and not an archive culture. His knowledge of Irish balladry was extensive and he wrote words for many folk airs (a few are included in this volume). Some of these, no doubt, are pastiche, but folk imagery and folk metres came readily and naturally to him, especially in his remarkable radio plays, where they often occur at moments of emotional tension or poignance.

Far stronger and more pervasive in his work than the folk element is the mythic one. As a young man he was deeply influenced by Yeats's dictum that the poet could employ myth as a vehicle of timeless wisdom, embodying universal truths about the psyche and about man's relationship with nature and with God (or the gods). But by temperament and background he was an earthier man, and there is a Dionysiac pulse in his language and rhythms which has its origins much less in intellectual aspiration than in a direct, powerful intuition of natural forces. While he had a mystical streak, it is not Platonic or transcendental; it is more a kind of psychic energy rooted in the earth, in myth, and the dualistic, creative-destructive forces of history.

It is not necessary to apologise for a writer's mythic preoccupations, or to suspect him of sculpting elaborate and fantastic ivory towers as a retreat from the contemporary world. Ivory towers can be excellent things in their way, and some of the best poetry and philosophy have come out of them, but Padraic Fallon did not find it necessary to construct one. His concern with mythic themes was neither a product of Forties Neo-Romanticism nor an afterglow of the Celtic Twilight (whose mythology, as exemplified by Yeats's *The Shadowy Waters*, was an afterglow of Pre-Raphaelitism and the twilight world of Maeterlinck and French Symbolism). It belongs firmly in one of the deepest and strongest twentieth-century currents. Joyce's *Ulysses* is composed over a ground-bass of Homeric references. Eliot's *The Waste Land* is a contrapuntal web of mythological themes, and so are large tracts of Pound's *Cantos*; David Jones's *In Parenthesis* sets the Welsh legend of the Battle of the Trees among the mud and blood of the trenches in the first World War. Even MacNeice, a darling of the "urban sensibility" school, was haunted by Greek and Biblical myths, and one of his very last poems, "Thalassa", is unmistakably an echo of the Odysseus theme. Robert Graves has provided a prose gloss on his poetic obsessions in that curious work *The White Goddess*. The mythic subjects and elements in Rilke's poetry are numerous; there are mythic references in most of the great Russian poets of the century, from Blok to Akhmatova and Tsvetayeva; the remarkable East German, Bobrowski, fills his "Shadow Land" with the ghosts of the old pagan Prussian and Lithuanian deities. And nearer home, poets as diverse as Sylvia Plath and Seamus Heaney have regarded myth and legend as active resources for poetry. In fact, it could even be said that this virtual obsession with myth and its special resonance is a modern *Leitmotiv*, one of the distinctive features of twentieth-century culture and totally different from the nineteenth-century approach, which rarely went beyond conventional salon "mythology".

Padraic Fallon was a searching but not a systematic thinker, a deeply-read man but not a scholar, and the mythic and philosophic elements in his work are more the fruit of eclecticism than of any process of ordered assimilation and study. These elements included Eastern philosophy and religion, both at first hand and indirectly through AE and Yeats; Gnosticism and Neoplatonism (again, partly a legacy from Yeats); the gynaeolatry of the Troubadours; elements from Frazer's *Golden Bough* and from Jung; Classical, Celtic and Oriental mythology; Christian symbolism combined with a rather un-Christian pantheism; and finally, a very twentieth-century sense of "dread" and impending catatrophe, which sometimes is at war with a serene inner fatalism. He was reasonably well grounded in the classics, though not a classical scholar like Graves or MacNeice, and in the last decade of his life he read and re-read his Latin poets, Horace particularly. His French was laboriously self-taught and strictly for reading, not conversation; but what natural insight he had into French poetry is shown by his Baudelaire, de Nerval and Mallarmé translations.

Fallon's immersion in Baudelaire and the Symbolists led him to Rimbaud, whose importance to many poets in the 1930s and 1940s lay largely in the fact that he was, broadly speaking, the link between Symbolism on the one hand and Surrealism and its tributaries on the other – and ultimately with the Neo-Romanticism of the 1940s, which has suffered unfairly because of its identification with the so-called Apocalypse movement. Along with his discovery (slightly later) of Rilke in J.B. Leishmann's translations, Rimbaud helped to set Fallon free from the inbred world of post-Revival Irish writing, and to turn him adrift on wider European waters. Rilke's influence can be seen as early as the poem "Virgin", written in 1946, and as late as "Lakshmi", written in 1967 (in which I seem to hear echoes of Rilke's "Spanish Dancer"), and it is almost too obvious in the intermittently impressive "Maud Gonne", in effect an elegy for a woman who was then still living. It was not the immaterial, allusive, introspective side of Rilke's poetry which primarily interested him, but his ability to "visualise" his poetry and to embody his subtlest intuitions in concrete imagery – a quality Rilke developed consciously under the influence of Rodin and the visual arts generally. This sculpturesque quality is strong in certain poems of Fallon's maturity, such as "A Public Appointment", which has the effect of a row of Greek bronzes or caryatids stirring to life.

In certain respects he could be said to have anticipated the swing back towards "pure" poetry so noticeable at the moment. This was largely a reaction against the loose, garrulous, journalistic verse so common in the last twenty-five years or so, much of it written by down-at-heel followers of Auden. Padraic Fallon did believe in the doctrine (perhaps ultimately Symbolist) that verbal sounds and rhythms are carriers of meaning; that poetry is a language in itself, sometimes quite independent of prose construction; and that genuine poetic imagery has organic life and self-sufficiency. Some of his late verse is extremely condensed and cryptic, a kind of self-communing or inner soliloquy without obvious reference to an audience. But on closer reading, such poems often turn out to have some definite, earthy, "realistic" context; the metaphysics have been set squarely in the West of Ireland mud.

When he died in Kent, he left by his typewriter a borrowed book of studies into religion in the ancient world; it lay open at a chapter on Gnosticism. On the typewriter itself was a translation of Rimbaud's "O Saisons, ô châteaux", two lines of which are engraved on his tombstone in Kinsale:

> I have made a magic study
> Of the good thing that eludes nobody.

> [J'ai fait la magique étude
> Du bonheur, que nul n'élude.]

– which perhaps is not exactly what Rimbaud meant, but presumably Padraic Fallon was aware of this. As they stand, these lines can be taken as a summation of a poetic odyssey of half a century.

This volume contains all the poems which appeared in the Dolmen Press *Collected Poems* of 1974 (now out of print and virtually unobtainable) and the Carcanet Press *Poems and Versions* of 1983. I have added some early poems which the poet excluded from the Dolmen volume, partly because they merit it and partly because this book would be unbalanced without them. A large selection of the incidental lyrics from his radio plays is also included, a few ballads, and some items which had been overlooked previously, such as the late translation of Baudelaire's 'L'Albatros'.

I acknowledge the help of the young poet-critic Peter Sirr in tracking down some elusive items, and of course the help and support of my five brothers, as well as the assistance of my own family in such practical matters as handling word-processors. And perhaps some belated acknowledgement is also due to the newspapers and periodicals in which many of these poems first appeared: *Agenda*, the *Bell*, *Botteghe Oscure*, the *Dublin Magazine*, the *Irish Times, New Statesman and Nation, New World Writing, PN*

Review, etc. A high proportion of them has vanished, like the half-forgotten or entirely forgotten poetry anthologies which included my father's work over the years. In the case of poems from plays, credit should be given to Radio Eireann (long ago subsumed into its Big Brother, Radio-Telefís Eireann), on which almost all of them were broadcast. I am also indebted to Seamus Heaney for his introduction.

BRIAN FALLON
Manor Kilbride, near
Blessington, Co. Wicklow

Notes

Gillies of Song; Tara, the ancient seat of the High Kings of Ireland, is in County Meath – an extra incentive for P.F. to dedicate the poem to F.R. Higgins, whose native country it was. The poem is typical of the romantic anti-clericalism of Fallon's generation of Irish writer-intellectuals in its idealised picture of pre-Christian, pagan Ireland and the rather simplistic blaming of religion for the nation's ills. (In fact, Tara's decline in the Christian centuries was due to political and not ideological causes.) There are also, of course, echoes of an older tradition – that of the medieval "Agallamh na Senórach", in which St Patrick and the aged Oisin argue endlessly from their irreconcilable viewpoints. For a recent revival of the tradition, *vide* Seamus Heaney's "Sweeney Astray" (Field Day Publications, Derry, 1983). "Ruadan" was a semi-legendary cleric, who ritually cursed Tara.

'Five provinces'; in ancient Ireland, "royal Meath" ranked as a province, along with Munster, Ulster, Leinster and Connacht. This tradition survives in the Gaelic word for province, *cúige*, which basically means "a fifth".

F.R. Higgins (1896-1941) was widely regarded in his lifetime as the finest Irish poet since Yeats, but is out of fashion today. He had a definite influence on P.F.'s early work, and P.F. wrote a lengthy elegy on his death, which he omitted from the *Collected Poems* and which I have omitted here.

Poète Maudit; Rimbaud was of course a potent influence on many writers in the 1940s, but Fallon's fascination with him went beyond fashion; he regarded him in effect as the archetype of the poetic vocation, the man chosen by the Muse almost against his conscious will. Rimbaud is *maudit* in two senses – first, by being singled out for the terrible gift of poetry, and secondly, by the curse he drew upon himself by denying it.

J'Accuse; written at the time of the Korean War, and the "general" is probably MacArthur, widely attacked at the time as a warmonger (he was, in fact, dismissed by President Truman for exceeding his powers in the theatre of war). It can, however, be taken as a generic picture of any warlord or militarist. The child is P.F.'s youngest son, Padraic (b.1946).

To One Newspaper Critic; probably addressed to a Dublin literary pundit of the 1950s who wrote under a number of pseudonyms – "Thersites", "Thomas Hogan" etc. A bibulous professional diplomat in private life, he is pilloried in O'Casey's *Autobiographies.*

Yeats's Tower at Ballylee; P.F. visited Thoor Ballylee in 1950 while on a motoring tour of the West of Ireland. It was then in a forlorn and dilapidated condition, but has since been fully restored. The war imagery refers to the outbreak of fighting in Korea, which seemed at the time an ominous and major step towards a third World War.

"Il Penseroso in the magic chamber"; a reference to Yeats's "Meditation in Time of Civil War":

> *Il Penseroso's* Platonist toiled on
> In some like chamber, shadowing forth
> How the daemonic rage
> Imagined everything.

Maris Stella; the scene evoked in the opening lines is just as P.F. could see it from the windows of his first-floor office in the Custom House in Wexford, overlooking the quays. *Maris Stella* is one of the traditional titles of the Virgin Mary, and of course countless seaside churches and sailing craft have been named after it.

Poem for my Mother; Killimore-Daly, in East Galway, is pronounced "Kill-eye-mer". The reference to Aughrim is to the battle of that name fought in 1691 – a far more decisive defeat for the Irish and Jacobite cause than the Battle of the Boyne in the previous year. According to a family tradition, a number of brothers who were ancestors of the poet's mother, Ellen Dillon, died in this battle. Whether Burkes or Dillons, they probably suffered in the massacre of the Irish infantry after the cavalry had virtually abandoned them.

Vowels; see Rimbaud's poem "Voyelles".

Dialogue Between Raftery and Death; the blind Gaelic poet Anthony Raftery (in Irish Antoine Ó Reachtabhra, Ó Reachtúire, or simply Raifteirí), who wrote in the first third of the nineteenth century, was very much a living legend in the countryside of Galway and Mayo during P.F.'s youth. His poems, which were first collected by Douglas Hyde early this century, are mostly broadsheet ballads, but a few are still anthology pieces and read by all Irish schoolchildren. He lost his sight at the age of nine, probably from an attack of smallpox, and the apparition of Death one night is supposed to have restored it briefly. Raftery died at the age of fifty-one, in Craughwell, a village or townland in which P.F. had several near relatives.

In real life Raftery seems to have been a troublesome and hard-drinking tramp rhymester, feared by the country people for his tongue and his satire (perhaps they remembered the old superstition that a poet's satires could raise blisters or other physical blemishes on his enemies). Fallon, however, simply used him as a symbolic figure of the blind poet-seer, half goliard and half Tiresias; he considered the real-life Raftery rather a poor poet. He made him the central character in his radio play *The Bell for Mr Loss*.

Maud Gonne; P.F. did in fact meet tête-à-tête the nationalist heroine, widow of John MacBride and Muse of Yeats. The poem appeared in the *Bell* magazine in February 1952, not long before her death.

A Flask of Brandy; a childhood memory of Athenry.

The Head; written in the early 1950s, this poem was lost and then found in the bottom of a drawer a decade later. The oracular imagery obviously relates to the Orpheus legend and also to the singing head of Bran – mythic themes which form the poetic plank of the radio play *The Vision of Mac Conglinne*.

Tradesman's Entrance; these lyrics are from the radio play *A Man in the Window*. Strictly speaking, this sequence should appear under "Poems and Plays", but as the poet included it in *Collected Poems*, I have preferred to let it stand.

First Love; again this is lifted from *Two Men with a Face*. As it has appeared already in *Collected Poems*, I have preferred to print it here rather than among "Poems from Plays".

Meeting and *Field Observation*: both based on real-life countrymen whom P.F. met almost daily while walking or driving into work from his house a few miles outside Wexford Town.

Johnstown Castle; a Gothic Revival building standing in spacious grounds a few miles from Wexford town, and now a State agricultural college. The "old lady" is its last private occupant, Lady Fitzgerald.

Wexford to Commodore Barry; written for the bicentenary of the birth of the Wexford-born sailor, one of the founders of the American navy. P.F. greatly admired the small bronze statue of Barry by Andrew O'Connor in the Municipal Gallery in Dublin, and on the occasion of his bicentenary (1957) urged the local authorities in Wexford to erect a lifesize version of it. Unfortunately his advice was ignored and they put up instead an inept and vulgar work by an obscure American sculptor, which still stands on the quays.

March TwentySix: written for the funeral in 1958 of his old friend, Seumus O'Sullivan (James Sullivan Starkey), poet, pundit, man of letters and founder-editor of the *Dublin Magazine*.

The River Walk; "Old Madge" is based upon a reminiscence told to the poet by his painter friend Tony O'Malley, who remembered her from his youth in Callan, Co. Kilkenny.

Weir Bridge; stone bridge over the Corrib river in Galway city, familiar to the poet from childhood. In "Closing Album" (1939) Louis MacNeice wrote of the same scene:

> Salmon in the Corrib
> Gently swaying
> And the water combed out
> Over the weir...

and George Moore in the "Salve" volume of *Hail and Farewell* describes how he, Yeats and Edward Martyn had watched the same sight a generation earlier.

Gowran Park; a racecourse in Co. Kilkenny, pronounced "Goran". Like other Irish writers of his generation, P.F. was a keen follower of the turf. (See "Curragh, November Meeting" on page 155.)

Fin de Siècle; obviously Yeats is meant.

The Young Fenians; this lyric is taken from a television documentary of 1966, commemorating the Fenian Rising a century before.

Capricornian; the poet was born under Capricorn (21 December to 19 January), a fact also alluded to in the poem "The House" (page 125). "That Old Poet"; Horace is meant – "....found spring wells holy"; the Bandusian spring, to which Horace vowed to sacrifice a kid (*haedus*). See Odes, Book III, Ode XIII. Of course there is also a reference to the "holy wells" found throughout Ireland, and to the lifegiving importance which springs of "sweet water" have for an island community.

A Visit West: written after a visit to Athenry during the 1960s. "Old Ben" was the poet's paternal uncle who was still living then, though ancient and bedridden. The Homeric image of the wooden horse symbolises the social revolution which has brought the one-time "wild Irish" inside the walls of a traditional Norman-English *Bürgerlich* town.

Boyne Valley; to my mind one of P.F.'s most profound poems, though at first the approach and even the theme may sound obscure. The river Boyne is famous in Irish history and legend and its lower reaches, in particular, are rich in ancient tumuli and prehistoric remains. The poem is a sustained meditation on the nature of myth and the ancient ritual of the sacrifice of a kingly victim on Midsummer Eve, thereby ensuring the success of the harvest and the survival of the tribe or nation, as well as the immortality of the priest-king himself. (Cf. Frazer's *Golden Bough*.) "Scantlings" were lopped poles or small tree-trunks used in building, before the advent of metal scaffolding. Cernunnos was an ancient Celtic (or Gaulish) god of the Underworld. "The barnacle" means the barnacle goose.

Kiltartan Legend; obviously Lady Gregory, rather than the wife of Odysseus, is the real subject of this poem.

Yeats at Athenry Perhaps; Coole House, where Yeats so often stayed as a guest of Lady Gregory, is half-an-hour's drive by car from Athenry, P.F.'s birthplace. Athenry (Gaelic *Áth na Rí*, "the ford of the kings") was a place of some importance in Norman-Irish and Elizabethan times and was sacked bloodily by Red Hugh O'Donnell during the Ulster Rebellion against Elizabeth. P.F. alludes several times to the great battle fought there in August 1319 between the Norman-English and Norman-Irish under Richard de Burgo and Richard de Bermingham, and the "native" Irish under Phelim O'Connor, the last Gaelic king of Connacht. O'Connor's heavy defeat, and his own pursuit and death, virtually ended Gaelic rule west of the Shannon. (Incidentally, on his mother's side the poet was related to the MacWilliam Burkes, those de Burgos who "went native" and adopted Gaelic names and customs.)
Juno's Peacock; another reference to Yeats's "Meditation in Time of Civil War".

Stop on the Road to Ballylee; the stop is at Ballinasloe, the town in Co. Galway where P.F. had been to boarding school many years before. The sight of mental patients shambling about in the asylum grounds leads him to see them as equivalents to the souls of the unburied dead in classical times, with rights neither in this world nor in Hades. (Beckett in his early novel *Murphy* takes a roughly parallel approach.) Interwoven with this, in a kind of irregular counterpoint, are memories of his schooldays and schoolfellows and of his first reading of Horace, who became a favourite writer in the last two decades of his life.
"The big tower" is obviously Yeats's, and he is quoted throughout. "mater saeva Cupidinum" (pitiless Mother of the sweet Loves) from Horace, Ode I, Book IV – the same ode, incidentally, which Yeats's friend Ernest Dowson quoted in the tag "non sum qualis eram bonae sub regno Cinarae".

"Three measures of clay and we're at liberty to leave"; a smuggled Horatian quotation. The reference is to Odes Book I, XXVIII, in which the ghost of a drowned sailor pleads for burial rites by the sprinkling of a few handfuls of sea-sand on his corpse:

> quamquam festinas, non est mora longa; licebit
> iniecto ter pulvere curras.

On the Tower Stairs; again the subject is Lady Gregory. Arthur Symon's reference to her as the *Strega* (witch) is documented in John Butler Yeats's letters, and for a quasi-humorous description of Yeats's magic-making activities, *vide* Moore's *Hail and Farewell*. Lady Gregory's family, the Persses of Roxborough, were well known in and around Athenry. "Bible household" – Lady Gregory's mother and sisters were ardent Protestant proselytizers. "Husband-father" – Augusta Persse was thirty-five years younger than her husband, Sir Robert Gregory of Coole Park, Gort. He had been Governor of Egypt as well as of Ceylon, and his friends included Gladstone, the historian Leckey and the archaeologist Layard. "Mr Gregory's postbag" – Sir Robert's grandfather had been under-secretary of State for Ireland, and she edited a selection of his correspondence as *Mr Gregory's Letter-box, 1813-1830*. She was not her husband's biographer, in fact; she edited his memoirs, which appeared posthumously. "That bronze" refers to Epstein's head of Lady Gregory.

The Small Town of John Coan; this sequence appears twice, but in such radically different versions that I have felt that I had no choice except to treat them as separate entities. Their origin is in Fallon's radio play, *Two Men with a Face* (in turn, a dramatisation of an early short story) in which a small-town businessman is curiously drawn towards a local halfwit in whom he recognises his own alter ego, his Doppelgänger. The central theme is the clash between reality and imagination, the man of the world who accepts "fact" and can cope with it, yet remains innately dissatisfied, and the halfwitted dreamer, the *Reine Tor*, who transcends and transfigures it. The later sequence, however, moves away decisively from this context. (See page 159.)

The House; the poet's birthplace in Athenry has been shortened by one storey, so that the room he was born in no longer exists. The lines

> Far East, Port Arthur and the yellow threat
> Of the little ricemen, battleships gone down

refer to the Russo-Japanese war and the fall of Port Arthur only a few days before P.F. was born. Wilhelm II of Germany harped on the "Yellow Peril" of the militant new Japanese empire, and urged the Western Powers to unite against it.

Magna Mater; "a dove plus an assenting virgin" refers to the traditional Christian imagery of the Incarnation, in which the Holy Ghost in the form of a dove swoops over the kneeling Virgin Mary. "The least erotic of the gods" is, of course, Christ. A smuggled Latin quotation occurs in the lines

> Where flowers are born with the names of kings
> You never heard of, pagan fellows...

which is an echo of Ausonius' much-anthologised description of souls wandering in the Underworld by spectral rivers –

> quorum per ripas nebuloso lumine marcent
> fleti, olim regum et puerorum nomina, flores.

For Paddy Mac; the poet Patrick Mac Donagh (1902-1961) was perhaps the closest of all P.F.'s literary friends. His sensitive, fastidious talent is unfairly neglected today, though there is a sympathetic note in Robert Hogan's recent *Dictionary of Irish Writers* and he continues to be represented in Irish anthologies.

Special for Nancy's Mother; written on the occasion of the marriage between Conor Fallon and Nancy Wynne-Jones in 1966. The wedding took place at the bride's family home near Dolgellau, and her two dead brothers (both killed in the Second World War) are the "gentle Lads" evoked as tutelary spirits.

Brigid Her Eve; the Feast of St Brigid, on 2 February, is still regarded in parts of rural Ireland as the beginning of spring, or at least the end of Winter (*Lá Fhéile Bríghde*), and her symbol, the rush cross, is hung over doors for good luck. In this poem the Christian saint is intermingled with the old pagan Brigid or Brigit or Bríde, the Celtic Muse, and with the Magna Mater/White Goddess who haunts P.F.'s entire output. The dedication is to his artist son Conor, and to his painter-wife, Nancy Wynne-Jones.

Lakshmi; suggested by an illustration in the *Larousse Dictionary of Oriental Mythology*, showing a bronze statue of the Hindu goddess. Lakshmi or Laksmi is usually depicted holding a lotus, and sometimes seated on an eight-leafed lotus throne. Originally an earth deity, she later became the goddess of health and good fortune. (See *The Illustrated Dictionary of Hindu Iconography* by Margaret Stutley.) My brother Conor now tells me that in the early 1960s his future wife, Nancy Wynne-Jones, gave P.F. a small bronze figure of Lakshmi, which he kept in his room.

Three Houses; Gurteen, Knockroe and Shanballard are all farmhouses where the poet stayed with near relatives in his childhood. "The Old Landleaguer" was an uncle by marriage on whom he based the character of Jerome in one of the finest of his radio plays, *The Poplar*.

Painting of My Father; the picture in question is by P.F.'s son Conor and was painted from memory. The poet's father, John Fallon, lived into his nineties, though deaf and with his sight failing. He had been a successful cattle and sheep 'jobber' until deafness ended his career, and P.F. recalls their trips together from Galway to the Dublin marts.

"The Broadstone, MGWR"; The old Broadstone station in north Dublin – a handsome neo-classical building – still stands but the Midland and Great Western Railway is long gone. The old Cattle Market has also vanished. "This strange hallucinatory land"; the poem was written when P.F. was living in Cornwall, near Penzance. "The Mount" is St Michael's Mount, which he could see from his window.

A Bit of Brass: as a schoolboy of eleven, Fallon witnessed the Irish Volunteers drilling around Athenry and their almost farcically inept effort at rebellion in 1916. This was less their fault than that of Eoin MacNeill, whose countermanding orders virtually confined the fighting to Dublin.

The Skellig Way; the Skelligs are a group of almost sheer rocks – they can hardly be called islands – off the Kerry coast, of which Skellig Michael is the biggest and best known. They are rich in monastic remains, some of which go back to the hermit-monks of the early Celtic Church. The name derives from the Gaelic word *Sceilg*, meaning a rock or cliff.

Dardanelles 1916; almost certainly P.F. has dated this poem a year too late, since by 1916 the fighting on the peninsula was virtually over and the Allied expedition had been withdrawn. The Connaught Rangers suffered heavily in the campaign, particularly in the fighting around the ill-famed "Hill 60" in August 1915, when bodies lay rotting in the torrid sun. One side-effect of the Dardanelles expedition was to have a lasting result on Irish history: one of the campaign's many discredited leaders, General Maxwell, was responsible for suppressing the Easter Rising in Dublin a few months later, and for the execution of its leaders.

Diarmuid and Gráinne was the first full-length radio play by Fallon to be broadcast by Radio Eireann, in the winter of 1950 (it was later performed on the BBC Third Programme, besides several revivals on the Irish station). One section was printed in the *Dublin Magazine* in 1951 and some of the lyrics have appeared separately. Slieve Echtge is the modern Slieve Aughty, a mountain in Mayo.

The Widowhood of Gráinne; after Diarmuid's death Gráinne marries Fionn, her old tormentor and the architect of her husband's death.
"...is a constellation"; Diarmuid here is equated with Thammuz-Adonis, who was placed among the stars by Venus after his death.

The Hags of Clough; one of Fallon's finest radio plays, exists in three versions, the first two in a mixture of prose and verse, the third almost entirely written in blank verse. The final version is easily the finest in terms of dramatic coherence and depth, but at least one of the earlier versions contains some excellent lyrics in the poet's quasi-folk vein. He seems to have thought them worth printing in their own right, since a manuscript in my possession shows revisions which he added in his own handwriting, and which I have followed.

The Seventh Step was a stage play in which Fallon experimented with a technique of verse interpolations set through realistic prose dialogue. The work impressed Irish critics when it was performed in Dublin and Cork in 1954, but though he rewrote it several times he eventually became dissatisfied with the play and virtually suppressed it. Some of the verse, however, he used later in other contexts.

Translations and Versions

Homeric Hymns; though a tolerable Latinist, Fallon did not know any Classical Greek. He worked chiefly from English versions in *The Oxford Book of Greek Verse in Translation*.
The Homeric Hymns are no longer attributed to Homer but to his followers and imitators. The fragment of Hesiod is from his *Theogony*.

Bellerophon; from Pindar's Olympian Ode XIII.

The Hyperboreans; from Pindar's Pythian X. The name means "Those (who dwell) beyond the North Wind" (*Boreas*).

The Infant Heracles; from Pindar's Nemean I.

Solvitur Acris Hiems; a translation, rather than a 'version', of Horace's Ode IV, Book I. It was written partly as a gesture of friendly rivalry towards the version by Louis MacNeice, which Fallon knew and admired.

Propertius to Ponticus; based very loosely on Propertius' Elegy VII, Book I, addressed to his friend Ponticus, an epic poet.

Confessio; this work by the so-called Archpoet (name unknown) is one of the most famous of all medieval Latin poems and has challenged numerous translators. Scholars have dated it roughly to the year 1169. It is, in effect, an *apologia pro vita mea* to the poet's powerful patron, Reinhold or Reginald von Dassel, archbishop-elect of Cologne and Chancellor to the Emperor Frederick Barbarossa, and was written in Pavia, Barbarossa's seat of rule in Northern Italy until his defeat by the Lombard League. As an ancient university town, famous particularly for its law faculty, Pavia was a place of resort for *scholastici vagantes* and, seemingly, for amorous dalliance. Louis MacNeice's version is much more condensed but does observe the so-called Goliardic metre – seven syllables followed by six.

Two Mallarmé Things for Sue; Sue (née Lurring) is the wife of P.F.'s son Ivan, and the poet occasionally sought her help when translating from French, because of her closer knowledge of the language. She has in her possession slightly different versions of these two pieces, given to her personally. I have preferred to use the present one because it was in the folder of completed poems left at his death; in literary merit there is nothing between the two.

O Saisons, O Châteaux; this translation is the last thing Fallon wrote and was on his typewriter when he died. The lucid and careful symbolism of the poem is discussed at some length in Enid Starkie's biography of Rimbaud, of which Fallon kept a copy. Two of the lines are engraved on his tomb near Kinsale. (See Afterword.)

Mary Hynes; for many years Fallon's most anthologised poem, is a fairly free rendering of Raftery's "Máire Ní hEidhin", also called "An Pabhsae Glégeal". He also took plenty of liberties with the same writer's "Caismirt an Phótaire leis an Uisge Beatha". The instant success of these two pieces recoiled on P.F. later, when the "revisionist" poets of the 1960s attacked the so-called Irish rural school; but in fact they are untypical of his work as a whole. ("Raftery's Dialogue with Death" is an original poem and was written later.) Incidentally, "Raftery's Dialogue with the Whiskey" was read several times by Dylan Thomas, without acknowledgement, during his reading tours of the United States. This fact only came to light when in 1963 Messrs Dent asked Fallon's permission to include the poem in the anthology *The Colour of Saying*, which greatly amused him.